a comma in a sentence

Other books by R. Gopalakrishnan

The Case of the Bonsai Manager
When the Penny Drops
What the CEO Really Wants from You

a comma in a sentence

Extraordinary Change in an Ordinary Family over Six Generations

R. GOPALAKRISHNAN

RAINLIGHT
RUPA

Published in RAINLIGHT by
Rupa Publications India Ltd 2013
7/16, Ansari Road, Daryaganj
New Delhi 110002

Sales centres:
Allahabad Bengaluru Chennai
Hyderabad Jaipur Kathmandu
Kolkata Mumbai

Copyright © R. Gopalakrishnan 2013

Foreword copyright © Mark Tully 2013

Front cover illustration inspired by a photograph courtesy
The Hindu archives.

All rights reserved.
No part of this publication may be reproduced, transmitted,
or stored in a retrieval system, in any form or by any means,
electronic, mechanical, photocopying, recording or otherwise,
without the prior permission of the publisher.

ISBN: 978-81-291-2977-2

First impression 2013

10 9 8 7 6 5 4 3 2 1

The moral right of the author has been asserted.

Typeset by Recto Graphics, New Delhi

Printed at Parksons Graphics Pvt. Ltd, Mumbai.

This book is sold subject to the condition that it shall not,
by way of trade or otherwise, be lent, resold, hired out,
or otherwise circulated, without the publisher's prior consent,
in any form of binding or cover other than that
in which it is published.

Dedicated to my father, G. Ramabadran
(a.k.a. Rajam), and my ancestors

I remember, I remember his dignified mien,
With a soul so gentle and a wit so sane,
I crave his presence, a balm for my soul,
'Tis twenty long years since Life took its toll.

Born in the year nineteen twelve,
Soon after the Titanic kissed the ocean shelves,
And a score of brave hearts along with Scott,
Scattered in the Antarctic with their brethren apart.

His respect for his parents could not obscure,
Nor his call to duty fails to assure,
A burning desire to make a mark,
And leave his loved ones, in the city to park.

With a quick mind and a formidable will,
Did the village schoolboy unsheathe his quill,
The supreme test of accounting skill,
Did he surmount, bare though his till.

His stride brisk, his bearing erect,
With poise and grace, and pride in his chest,
His face glistening with emotion and appeal,
His voice intense with concern for the sequel.

He nursed in him a hunger to learn,
About all and sundry, no matter what they earn,
His eyes moistened at the plight of the poor,
Much did he stretch, to help them for sure.

Six healthy children did he sire,
Of their education and development he did not tire,
I think he would have been pleased if he had seen,
His offspring, his legacy their inability to wean.

'Father, dear father' my heart cries out,
The silence is deafening, of that there is no doubt,
I know from his heavenly abode, he watches his offspring,
With a smile and affection, forever doting in the wings.

This poem was composed by my older brother,
R.V. Raghavan.

Contents

Foreword ix
Preface xiv

Tanjore in the Nineteenth Century	1
World within a Civilization	5
Fighting the British	13
Battle at Delhi	22
Famine around the Rice Bowl	28
Obscure Controversy	38
Rising Challenge of Caste	43
Dawn of the Twentieth Century	50
The Lure of Calcutta	57
The Great Metropolis	70
Emergence of the Professional	76
Raising a Family	84
A Wonderful Childhood	95
Episodes that Touched Me	105
Maturing into Adulthood	114
Joining Hindustan Lever	124
Lessons from Experience	132
LPR to LPG in the Twenty-First Century	144
Looking Ahead	152

Foreword

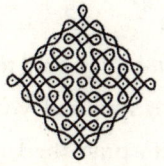

I first met the author, Gopal, as I came to know him, when he was sitting behind a spacious desk set in his tastefully but unostentatious office in Bombay House, the headquarters of India's largest business conglomerate, Tata. On that occasion I described him as 'nattily dressed, with his matching shirt and tie, fashionable rimless spectacles, and neatly trimmed graying hair'. He seemed every inch a top modern executive. That impression was confirmed by the staccato but polite sentences in which Gopal talked and his mastery of all aspects of the highly varied twenty-seven publicly listed companies in the Tata group.

The next time I met Gopal he was emerging from the changing room in Mumbai's Bombay Gymkhana after playing tennis, before heading for work. He was greeted by several members and was clearly popular and respected. Yet this executive—who has succeeded outstandingly in the highly competitive world of two multinational conglomerates, and is totally at home in the top echelons of Mumbai society who are to be seen in the Gymkhana club—does not come from a privileged background.

He and others in his generation were the first members of the family to get a university education, and his father and uncle were the first to move out of their traditional village in the deep south of India.

In *A Comma in a Sentence*, Gopal tells the story of his family over the last almost two hundred years and six generations. Until Gopal's grandfather's time, the Tamil Brahmin family were small-time landowners, some of whom became temple priests. They were perfectly satisfied with traditional village life but, even in those days, had to cope with change. Coping with change becomes the main theme of this family history. It could be called subaltern history because it's the story of typical people of their times, the story of how the family gradually came out of the isolation of village life into the world, and succeeded there.

This is not a rags to riches story. There are no sensational twists and turns. But it's nonetheless fascinating for that. The six generations accepted and adapted to change, took advantage of new developments, and yet were not swept off their feet. As Gopal says, 'Each generation felt concerned about how the next generation would cope with change. But the next generation coped marvelously.'

The pace of change accelerated from generation to generation. In the early years of the nineteenth century, Gopal's family lived in a village where villagers were not much concerned about who their rulers were because the arm of the state was not long enough to reach them. As the railways spread and newspapers began to be published, the remote village of Vilakkudi, in the rice bowl of Tanjore, became less isolated from the rest of India. News which used to be spread by word of mouth from town to village, and was often severely distorted before it even left the town, was now authenticated and spread by the new media. The information they brought made villagers more concerned about their rulers. Gopal's great grandfather questioned the justice of British rule when he compared the Indians who died in the Madras famine with the news he had heard about the British feasting at a function to celebrate the proclamation of Queen Victoria as the Empress of India.

Gopal's grandfather realized that changes in education had to be accepted. Members of the family had taken pride in the Brahmin tradition that the importance of memory in gaining knowledge is supreme. Without denigrating the value of this tradition and the knowledge that came with it, Gopal's grandfather realized that modern schooling was essential if his children were to be adequately prepared for life in the new, fast-changing world. So, he arranged for Gopal's father, Rajam, to go to a nearby elementary school, and from there he was sent to a high school.

Gopal's father and his brother were the generation that realized they must take advantage of the opportunities offered by India's burgeoning cities and so moved out of the village. In the village, they would have spent their lives farming three crops a year, and being involved in the village temple, perhaps even becoming priests as earlier generations had done. But agriculture was becoming less and less of a paying proposition. Moving out was not that simple. It required the permission of one's elders. But once again the older generation had the wisdom to appreciate that change must be embraced. The patriarch of the family was Rajam's uncle and he was persuaded that the young man was genuinely committed to making a go of it in Calcutta and gave him his blessing.

When Rajam reached Calcutta he did not forsake the traditions of the family. He lived in a joint family with his brother and his cousin. They all sent money back to their village. Although he had no degree, Rajam did get an accountancy qualification and this was the basis on which he built a successful career in business from nothing. Rajam realized that the next generation, Gopal and his five other siblings, would need to take their formal education further. He saw to it that Gopal was sufficiently well educated to gain admission to one of the prestigious Indian Institutes of Technology, the ambition of almost every Indian student bent on a scientific or technological career. Now Gopal and his brother have taken their children's education one step further. All their children have degrees, and the degrees are from prestigious international universities like London and Harvard.

There is an underlying message in this saga of a family's journey through the last two hundred years, and it is a message that Gopal passes on to all of us who are buffeted by the winds of change: 'Progress means holding onto the core values and letting go of the frills, accoutrements, and symbolism.'

So Gopal still lives by the core values held by his great-great grandfather, whose world was restricted to his village. One of the turning points in his father's life was his decision that his Brahmin pigtail did not fit in with the successful career he was trying to build in Calcutta. Realizing it was what Gopal would call an accoutrement, Rajam dispensed with it. But he did not dispense with the values of his family traditions. Gopal discusses those values and ends his book, saying 'The greatest treasure we can leave for our children is not wealth but *sanskar* (family values)—the more of us who can do so, the better society will be.' Many would say our society is so discontented and disturbed because there is not sufficient respect for family values, and tradition is too casually swept aside. *A Comma in a Sentence* is the history of one family's handing on traditional values over six generations, and that gives it a particular relevance today when, to quote a priest I once heard, 'we seem to be drunk on change'.

London   Sir Mark Tully
28 July 2013

Preface

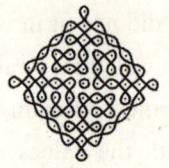

Every narration in this book is real, based on real characters. My grandfather's grandfather, Ranganathan, was born around 1824. This book traces the evolution of our family from that period. In the interests of narrative continuity, I have traced the descendants of Ranganathan via his son, Ooshi, and my father, Rajam, onwards to the next generation.

Nineteenth and twentieth century colonial Indian society evolved differently than those of Europe and America. During the 1850s, Europe was experiencing what history has come to recognize as the spring of nations. France, Germany, Italy, Poland, the Austrian Empire, all experienced revolt against their leaderships. America was torn between the Unionists and the Confederates, and held together by a lion-hearted Abraham Lincoln. Our village was sequestered, not just from such global events but even from much of what was happening within India.

Unlike western countries where birth and death registries and church records exist, in India we have no such records. I was born in 1945 and I do not possess a birth certificate! Therefore, I could access only limited personalized family information. And this is why I relied on anecdotal information and considerable background reading. I have been gathering information on this subject for over thirty years and have thus accumulated many stories narrated by family elders.

My father belonged to a family of seven siblings: older brother Srinivasan, younger brothers Krishnan and Sampath and younger sisters Champaka Lakshmi, Lakshmi and Padmasini. Of that generation, only one or two are alive today. My aunt, Janaki Krishnan, the wife of Krishnan, has been an invaluable source of information.

Indian society has evolved over thousands of years. In this context, two hundred years is a relatively short period. The period covered in this book more or less coincides with the peak and the decline of the British Empire in India.

India's history and culture are so rich that the entire British Raj is a mere speck in an evolving story. Depending on how you view them, the relative insignificance of historical events brings to my mind the principle derived by the sixteenth century Polish astronomer, Nicolaus Copernicus. His work showed that the earth is not at the centre of the universe. From a physics perspective, humans play no special role in the cosmos, they are only part of a larger narrative. In the same spirit, our family's narrative is set amidst the social, economic and political evolution of society as experienced by them over two centuries. My ancestors and family members are incidental to the narration—they are characters through whom the anecdotes are told.

While reading this book, the reader will get a flavour of the times. The huge social change that evolved in Indian villages over this period is sought to be brought out evocatively through the experiences of one family. Some imagination has been used as the sauce to hold the real anecdotes together.

Two characters stand out—the extrovert Ooshi Veera Raghavan (*b*. 1859), my father's grandfather, and the spirited Rajam (*b*. 1912), my father.

The title of the book has been inspired by the distinctive status of a comma in grammar—it has an apparently lowly position, but is still very meaningful; hence, *A Comma in a Sentence*.

My family belongs to the Vadagalai Iyengar Brahmin sect. According to a study in Andhra Pradesh, all the Vadagalai Iyengars had a genetic similarity (rhesus-d gene frequency) to the people of Faisalabad, now in Pakistan. If the Indo-Aryan migration story is to be believed, this fact may be one more piece in the assembly of the jigsaw. Who knows?

My family had roots in rural India. It hailed from a really small village—Vilakkudi in the Tanjore area of South India. Even today the village has a population of only about four thousand people.

My generation has been the first to get college degrees. My elder brother was the first in our family to go abroad for studies, while my elder sister was the first woman in our family to acquire a college degree. These facts are viewed with great surprise by our children who have been raised to take university and foreign education for granted.

This book came into being because of my strong compulsion that this story just had to be told. This urge faintly resembles the passion and spirit of George Mallory, who repeatedly climbed Mount Everest 'because it is there' and Sir Ernest Shackleton, who explored the Antarctica because it had not been fully explored.

My ideas about the target readers kept evolving as the story developed. Initially, I thought it would be my endowment for the future generations of our family. My paternal grandparents, Gopalan and Sundaravalli of Vilakkudi, had six children, over thirty grandchildren and, as per my last count, almost one hundred great grandchildren, who have now started their own families. Hence, the children and grandchildren of our family's next generation would be one interested segment. In the societies in which they will live and grow in the twenty-first century, it would, in all likelihood, be interesting for them to be aware of their roots, what it means to them in terms of values and then figure out where they wish to take their families.

I also sensed intuitively that other Indians would find it an interesting read as a surrogate for their own family histories, which may not have been committed to paper. The contents of this book may or may not represent a long-term sociological trend, but the narrative is the archetype of the story of millions of modern Indian families.

The book would be of interest to a wider audience, too—those interested in an anecdotal mixture of the sociology, economics and history of our society. When a society is undergoing change, people seldom realize how big these changes are. At times, it helps to step back from the microscopic details and see the bigger picture.

Anecdotes are not a bad way to view history. This account is a subaltern view of how events transpired; a view of how India and the world looked and changed from the perspective of our little village. I do not attempt a scholarly piece of researched history. I have tried to set each era of the last six generations within the social mores of the time.

I have no scholarly pretensions with respect to social science, economics or politics. I have tried to tell a story which is part history, part sociology, part family anecdotes but, above all, entertaining and insightful. The reader, I hope, will have the feeling of being in conversation with the author while reading this narrative.

After all, the great epics and philosophies of India have all come to us through word of mouth.

During my student days, I had read R.K. Narayan's *Malgudi Days* comprising a bunch of stories about life in a fictional village called Malgudi. I loved its simplicity of style and the narratives. The same style has influenced me in writing this book.

I also read Prakash Tandon's *Punjabi Century* after I joined Hindustan Lever as a management trainee in 1967.

Later in 1974, I was inspired by Alex Haley's hugely successful tome, *Roots*.

I mention these facts as acknowledgement of inspiration, but refrain from suggesting any equivalence with those wonderful books.

There are many I should thank for their contribution to this manuscript. First, my wife, Geeta, who conceptualized the cover design based on her inspiration from her native Srirangam *agraharam* and a photograph from the archives of *The Hindu*. The design department of Rupa Rainlight rendered the concept brilliantly. Second, my children, Anugraha, Anirudha and Anila. They are the reason for my writing the book. They gave me terrific inputs and feedback. I owe thanks to my parents, who were both hugely inspirational to me and my siblings. The Brihadaranyaka Upanishad verse is an appropriate epigraph for exemplifying my dear parents' lives:

Asato maa sadgamaya (lead me from untruth to truth)
Tamaso maa jyotirgamaya (lead me from darkness to light)
Mrtyormaa amrtam gamaya (lead me from death to eternity)

I thank my uncles, aunts and the extended family for their painstaking narration of various events from the hoary past. Some of my relatives and friends contributed by making important suggestions and changes in the early drafts: Sudha Raghavendran, Ashok Vasudevan, Gopal Srinivasan, B.K. Narayan, V.G. Veeraraghavan, S. Raghavan and my five siblings—Jaya Krishnan, R.V. Raghavan, Saroja Sathyam, R. Narayanan and R. Srinivasan.

Non-Tamil friends—Indians and foreigners—also advised, very willingly and generously, suggestions to widen the scope and the potential footprint of interest in the book: journalist Anil Dharker, Tata colleague Mathai Joseph, Distinguished Fellow of Carnegie Mellon Oopali Operajita, former Unilever colleague Brian Dive, Sir Mark Tully and *The Economist*'s India correspondent Patrick Foulis.

I must thank my publisher, Rupa Rainlight. Ritu Vajpeyi-Mohan has been a consistent supporter. But for her efforts and encouragement, I do not know whether this would have become a real book. The team at Rupa Rainlight has worked diligently to produce a book that is of great sentimental value to me, but more importantly I hope, of wider interest. Thanks to Rupa Rainlight for bringing to life a project that I began in 1984 and completed only in 2013.

Tanjore in the Nineteenth Century

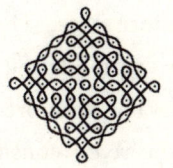

The southern part of India has had a somewhat cloistered history compared to the rest of the country. When compared to the triangle below the Vindhya mountains, the rest of the country has been ravaged by invasions, wars, revolutions and social change on a significant scale. The deeper one goes into the south, the more sheltered the area becomes.

This historical fact has many consequences, two of which are worth mentioning: first, that Vedic tradition and orthodoxy are thought to have been well preserved in the south. Over the last two centuries, southern religious practices and social customs have been widely perceived as being authentic. Second, as a result of clinging to tradition, the south has an image of being conservative and averse to change. Even as late as the 1900s, Madras was perceived as not being brushed by the political turmoil of Delhi, the commercial vigour of Bombay or the social activism of Calcutta.

Many parts of the country presented a spectacle of brown lands eagerly waiting for the southwest monsoon on which the fortunes of the people depended. Not so in Tanjore.

Blessed to have the downstream flow of the Cauvery, Tanjore was awash with fresh water. For centuries, the Cauvery, originating in Coorg and flowing eastwards at a gentle gradient, flowed through the Tanjore area. The river created a delta around Tanjore before surrendering its torrential waters into the Bay of Bengal. The Tanjore lands benefitted from the rich silt carried by the river, considered holy—the Ganga of the south! The land produced abundant crop without the uncertainties of war or weather. The pain experienced in many other parts of the country was alien to the people of Tanjore.

In Madras, a thousand miles to the south of the country, far from the Gangetic plains, the heat is searing. Because of its proximity to the equator, much of Tamil country experiences hot weather throughout the year; people have neither experienced nor have any concept of winter. There are two seasons: very hot summer and hot summer, year after year. But oh, it is so pleasant when the northeastern monsoon arrives every year during the months of Aipasi and Kartikai, approximating to November.

An aerial view of the landscape of Tanjore in those days would have revealed a sea of lush green with little enclaves spatially tucked away into the green. These enclaves housed hamlets, inhabited by people who led an idyllic life amidst the rich bounty of nature. Most villages sprung up on the banks of the Cauvery or its tributaries, surrounded by swaying coconut trees, banana plantations, succulent food crops and temples galore.

From the late 1680s until the early 1850s, the area was ruled by the Tanjore Marathas. At the apogee of the Maratha reign, Tanjore was a cradle of music, dance and fine arts, well known all over the south—a legacy that continues to this day.

The decline began in the 1800s. A witness has written poignantly, 'It was most painful to see this slow but sure grinding of good, noble and generous men and women, whose only fault was that the new times sprang upon them with lightning speed and they were not alert enough to save themselves.'

Maratha rule ended in 1855 with the death of the last Tanjore Maratha, Sivaji, who died without an heir. This Sivaji was not the great and famous Maratha warrior—he was reported to be quite sickly, but nonetheless had twenty wives! After his death, the British, who were well established in India, assimilated Tanjore into the Madras Presidency.

Village life was dominated by the Brahmins who had a reputation for being scrupulously clean and extremely spartan in their habits. Even a wealthy Brahmin family would present an utterly simple home, unlike the lavish contemporary mansions of the wealthy in Bengal or Bombay.

The Brahmins devoted themselves to the study of Sanskrit and Tamil religious literature, the propagation of tradition, the upkeep of temples and offering temporal advice to the people around them. In those days, the Brahmins were meant to be priests, and priests they were. They were also expected to inherit their profession. If an exigency forced them to change, they stepped sideways into related occupations like becoming cooks or offering manual services in the temples.

The views and values of any community are shaped by many things such as family, gender, ethnicity and generational experience. Having a clear-eyed view of the past helps a community or a family to understand where they are, what was right or wrong and the reasons for that state. Such knowledge, of course, turns out to be a hindrance if it results in producing bigots or orthodoxies.

In societies around the world, some form of caste, usually based on occupation, has existed. That is, every society had some hierarchy based on the prevailing social and political milieu. This is because when it comes to economic interests, we are invariably guided by personal gain. But when it comes to social interests, we are guided by values and ideas. India, as everybody knows, has been no different, perhaps to an extreme.

However, caste hierarchies become vulnerable when they become immutable or less than inclusive. Unconstrained rule by any single caste has the seeds of change built into it. The impact of Brahmin hegemony was played out in Tanjore and elsewhere in the Tamil country during the early part of the last century. The ancestral history in this book touches upon this history.

My native village of Vilakkudi was a small hamlet of three thousand people in the lush and green Tanjore area—it is still a small village, now with four thousand people.

World within a Civilization

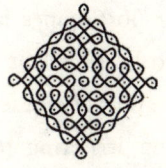

It was a hot summer afternoon in the middle of 1857. The sun was beating down mercilessly on the plains of Hindoostan, not uncommon for this time of year.

Ranganathan, who turned thirty-three that year, lay down on the *thinnai* (front porch) of his house after his midday meal. He had two implements to enable a peaceful afternoon siesta—his *angavastram* (upper-body cloth) and his *vishiri* (hand fan).

His wife, Ranganayaki, was from neighbouring Rayanallur. She was well trained in culinary arts—he felt sated with the traditional meal of rice served with *kuzhambu, shathu-amudu* and *thair*. Ranganayaki was not only a wonderful cook, she was a great partner in many respects. They had been married for several years; in fact, he was unsure exactly how long. Both of them had been very young when they were married. She had already borne him three children; she took active interest in matters concerning them, and made an almost perfect wife for him. She was soft-spoken, unlike the argumentative wife of Krishna next door.

What more could one expect from a good wife other than this deep and abiding partnership? Ranganathan counted Ranganayaki as one of his greatest assets. In fact, the astrologer who had examined their horoscopes had proclaimed that the match would turn out to be excellent.

The day was sultry and very quiet. The fly kept buzzing around his head, annoying, irritating and almost overpowering Ranganathan. Ranga, as he was called by his friends, swiped vigorously before covering his head with the *angavastram*.

'What a world God created,' he thought. 'Here I am, a fairly tall person, certainly by the standards of my own community, and a fly, a tiny fly, is capable of making my life so uncomfortable.' Through the hazy swathes of hot air rising from the *agraharam* (Brahmin quarters), he perceived a deeply philosophical point in the thought. After all, when infected or disabled, the smallest body parts produced the greatest discomfort; similarly, minor points of difference with a wife can lead to unnecessarily vociferous altercations.

'Such is life,' he mused.

His heroic attempts to swat the fly were singularly unsuccessful. In fact, his efforts to keep the fly at bay made him even more tired than he might have been otherwise.

Ranga's half-asleep mind drifted lazily to his childhood years. He was proud to have been raised right here in Vilakkudi. He knew his birth star in terms of Tamil astrology, he was unsure how it corresponded to the new English calendar. His best guess was that he was born around 1824.

Life in his village was fairly self-sufficient. Most of the events that interested him occurred in and around Vilakkudi, or its satellite, Rayanallur. Life seemed quite independent of whatever happened outside the village surroundings.

About six years before this hot afternoon, Ranga recalled, the *vellai karan* (white man) had started something called a census, a new practice of counting the number of people in the village. To Ranga it appeared unnecessary, and certainly quite useless. However, the *tehsildar* (local revenue official) had subsequently told the villagers that there were about three thousand people living in Vilakkudi and Rayanallur. Ranga never understood how his life could change as a result of this knowledge.

Ranga knew that a few villagers owned land while the majority worked on the land as labour. Almost everyone's occupation in the village was land-related. The Cauvery provided plenty of water for agriculture, and Ranga could extract as many as three crops of paddy each year. In fact, the *tehsildar* often described the area around Vilakkudi as the rice bowl of the whole of Madras! The high point of successful farming was the annual *Pongal* festival, which occurred at the end of the month of *margazhi* (approximately mid-January).

Ranga mulled over his daily routine, a very busy one. It included numerous baths, the collection of flowers and *tulsi* leaves, the *sandhya vandanam* (puja) three times a day, the *pariseshanam* (thanksgiving) before every meal, and other such rituals taught to him by his father. Although the Brahmins lived in their own enclaves, they occupied a very high position in village society. They maintained their houses scrupulously, which meant washing the floors periodically with cow dung (which, incidentally, was used as a disinfectant). Owing to their *acharam* (religious rituals), Brahmins accepted neither food nor water from non-caste Hindus. Since the Brahmins occupied the highest temporal positions, they probably regarded other castes as inferior.

Poor Brahmins were employed as cooks by the Jesuits in the bigger towns of the Madras Presidency because Brahmins were known to cook light and clean food. To maintain their balance of mind and equanimity, the Brahmins avoided liquor at all costs. In fact, to the Brahmin, drinking liquor was considered a vice.

Ranga was aware that other communities perceived the Brahmins quite differently. Once, when he had visited the town of Mannargudi some twenty miles away, he heard about a controversy. A Jesuit priest had said very favourable things about the simplicity and the clean habits of the Brahmins. However, he went on to express the view that the Brahmins were proud and arrogant. There had been considerable commotion after this incident, but luckily it died down quickly.

So far as Ranga knew, the pattern of his life followed, more or less, that of his father and grandfather. The family was not poor, but by no means was money easy to come by.

Not much seemed to change in his village. The farmers grew pulses and vegetables for home consumption and paddy for the market. They kept aside several *mootais* (bags of paddy) for personal use during the year and sold the surplus paddy for cash. He or his fellow farmers would never buy paddy in the market as it was considered a sign of penury. Two cows dutifully provided milk for consumption at home, rich dung for manure as well as feed for the kitchen fire.

A typical day would involve hard physical work in the field, visits to the market centre, conducting religious functions—thread ceremonies and marriage—and participation in village planning. The village was a bit like a modern-day cooperative society, though it was genuinely cooperative!

The high point of the day was the *aradhana* at the Sri Kasturi Ranga temple just behind his house. In particular, he recalled relishing the *shundal* and *sheera* (temple snacks) served at the temple after the evening prayers to the Lord. In the absence of daylight, most activities, other than chatting, ended by 6 p.m.

There was no formal school, but there was a *vadyar mama* (schoolteacher uncle) who conducted a few classes for the Brahmin boys. Most of the education was religious in nature. Family expectations from education demanded that the young son acquire a level of proficiency in Sanskrit—the language of the Vedas, as well as Tamil—the language of the Kural from the *Sangam* period. The Tamil language was known to predate Sanskrit.

Ranga felt that he truly belonged here. His universe was actually the *agraharam*, not even the village, let alone the far-away cities of Madras or Tanjore. The social mores were well established and administered by the village elders. He thought that it was a people's rule, irrespective of whether the ruler was a Tanjore Nayak or a *vellai karan*.

The fly buzzed past his ears making a screeching sound. He flayed his *angavastram* in the air in response. Such a small fly, but such a nuisance!

As an adolescent, Ranga had accompanied his father to the temple in Uttiramerur near Kanchipuram. To his great interest, he was shown a *kallivettu* (stone inscription) that described the governance of the area. It was administered through a system of local democracy. Normal disputes were settled within the village. There was very little concept of the 'outside world'; the social system was self-sufficient. Arbitration was quick, cheap and useful in its own way. As it operated in those times, the justice system was administered with fairness.

The village folk had become immune to who ruled and from where—the Cholas, the Nayaks or the Marathas. Dynasties came and went, but the people went on forever.

Health was given by God and ill health was cured by Him. He recalled the death of one of his aunts several years ago. It was not a pleasant sight for his youthful eyes. She gradually shrivelled up and died, and young Ranga was never sure what she died of. A *nattu vaidya* (local medicine practitioner) administered some medicine, but to no avail.

The community had been good and fair to him as he had been appointed the priest of the temple in the *agraharam*. He was thirty-three, and would have the opportunity to serve the community through his ministrations at the Sri Kasturi Ranga temple for perhaps another twenty years. This would augment his family income from agriculture. To him and his family, the appointment as priest at the temple was an important accomplishment.

The fly buzzed past his tonsured head once more in supreme defiance of his active efforts thus far. For a moment he was furious, and howled in rage. From an inner room, Ranganayaki shouted to ask what was afflicting him so much as to make him scream so loudly. Nothing, he bawled back.

The heaviness of slumber on a hot afternoon won the battle, his eyelids drooped again. So, come again, what was passing through his mind? Ah yes, his appointment to the prestigious post of priest at the Vilakkudi temple.

The temple, he had been told by his father, dated back at least a hundred years, to the 1700s. As a youngster, he had been in awe of the fact that many Vedic scholars had emerged from this blessed temple. He considered himself blessed to have secured the role of priest, a position he could serve till his midfifties. His father had died at the age of approximately sixty, so how much more time would the Lord give him? He would wait out his time.

Ranga remembered the fanfare and the glamour of temple festivals; in particular, the *panguni uttiram* festival. Every year, all temples around Vilakkudi would celebrate *utsavams* (festivals), the famous ones being at Mannargudi, twenty miles to the northwest and at Nagapattinam, some twenty miles to the east of Vilakkudi.

In the heart of Nagapattinam was the Sundararaja Perumal temple. The temple was very old; actually, all the temples in the vicinity of Vilakkudi were believed to be very old. The Nagapattinam temple had an idol of Adisesha (serpent god) and both the temple and the festival were famous for several hundred miles around.

His knowledge of the happenings outside his immediate environment came principally from his visit to the market. For routine matters, a trip to Kottur or Thiruthuraipoondi would suffice, but for special things, he had to go to Mannargudi. Now, this was a trip that could take him three or four hours on foot or by bullock cart. It certainly had to be something important to warrant the long journey to Mannargudi.

Having gone to the Kottur market to sell some *mootais* (bags) of paddy, Ranga was disturbed by some vague and unauthenticated information he heard: that there was some sort of revolution going on somewhere he could vaguely identify as being far away to the *vadakku* (north), in Delhi. The story went that Indian soldiers had killed British officers and had installed the *tulaqa* (Muslim) king, Bahadur Shah Zafar again.

His mind did not wish to analyse the news he had heard. So what if there was a revolution in Delhi! His life would carry on and the tehsildar would be back ever so often to collect a share of paddy as taxes. His life was in Vilakkudi and the cool waters of the Cauvery in whose arms his village was nested.

His eyelids drooped once again, and this time he was not bothered by the fly.

Fighting the British

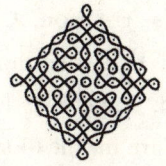

A couple of months later, Ranga needed to make a trip to Mannargudi. Since it would take many hours, his mind was free to think about matters that he normally would not reflect on. He ruminated on what he had heard—that indeed there were major developments in the north. It was confirmed that Indian soldiers were fighting English soldiers. Word had it that the feeble Bahadur Shah Zafar had been requested to lead the fight against the *vellai karan*. Ranga would have to wait until he reached Mannargudi to authenticate this information as there were too many confusing rumours in Vilakkudi.

Ranga's eight-year-old son, Veera Raghavan, accompanied him to Mannargudi for the first time. He was exceptionally tall and wiry, and consequently nick named Ooshi (needle), and was, later in life, regularly referred to as Ooshi Veera Raghavan. It is funny how pet names stick, because Veera's whole lineage, including myself, came to be known in the village as Ooshi descendants.

Veera Raghavan was an extrovert, extremely chatty and curious. He wanted to know the names of the villages they walked past, what their special features were, what kind of people lived there and so on. He kept asking the preoccupied Ranga a whole host of questions on a range of subjects, sometimes to the latter's irritation. Checking this irritation, Ranga reminded himself that one should not discourage or quieten the young mind, something he had learnt from his father. Fathers and sons are meant to spend time together and have meaningful conversations. And, thus, Ooshi and Ranga proceeded to Mannargudi.

Ranga did not understand war, let alone how a reportedly feeble king could lead it. His long walk enabled him to recall a few discussions and anecdotes he had heard as a child: village elders talking about Indians fighting the foreigners. It was all a bit confusing.

'*Appa,* who is this *vellai karan*? Why has he come to our country? Is there any caste among the *vellai karan*?' asked little Ooshi.

Ranga explained that there were several categories among the foreigners, just as we have Brahmins, Vellalars, Chettiars and Nadars among our people. They looked similar, but had different practices and habits. Some were called English, others French, some others were called Dutch. To him, they were all *vellai karan*. He really could not appreciate or explain why these people had left their faraway countries and were fighting wars in someone else's country. There must obviously be something valuable in or around this country that encouraged the white man to come and fight here!

Almost a century and a half later, the economist Angus Maddison would collate data to validate that the second most prosperous nation in the world during Ranga's time was India!

'*Appadiya*? When did the *vellai karan* arrive in our lands?' asked Ooshi. Ranga explained what he had learned as a child: that the *vellai karan* had established rule successfully in Madras at a place called Fort St. George, at a time when the Tanjore Maratha had become too weak to rule. So there was no fight or battle. In fact, according to Ranga's information, 'Madras had long ago become a part of England and their village, Vilakkudi, was being ruled from Fort St. George.'

Ranga's life was largely indifferent to whether his village was ruled by the English, the Madurai Nayaks or the Tanjore Marathas. However, there seemed to be one noticeable difference: there were certainly far fewer wars and less strife during Ranga's lifetime when compared to that of his father's. Ranga's father had told young Ranga horrendous tales about bloodshed and war, and he recalled particularly the stories of the Poligar chief, Katta Boman, the great battle by Tipu Sultan and the sacrifices of the young men during the Vellore uprising.

'*Shollikite pongo* (keep talking), *appa*. Tell me more, lots more,' piped the young Ooshi enthusiastically.

He recalled the story of Katta Boman most vividly. The village elders recounted it as inspiring history from their own childhood. Katta Boman was a *pallayakarar* chief from Tirunelveli, further south. The English people, unable to pronounce his caste, simplified it to Poligar. Katta Boman fought the imposition of English rule furiously till, finally, with their stronger arms, the English captured this hero. Katta Boman was mercilessly hung by the neck, recalled Ranga's father; at that time, Ranga had not been born and his father himself was a young man.

Another story passed down the generations in the village was about Tipu Sultan, the great king of Mysore. He led a war against the English at about the same time that Katta Boman was fighting the English in the Tirunelveli area. There was fierce fighting at a place near Mysore called Srirangapatna. The valorous Tipu was killed as he defended his fort in that city.

Srirangapatna was a town of religious importance to *vaishnavas* like Ranga. Several centuries earlier, a *vaishnava* temple had been consecrated at Melkotai, near this town, by Sri Ramanuja, the patron saint of his community, the Iyengar Brahmins. This emotional connect with Srirangapatna made the killing of Tipu Sultan even more poignant in the mind of the deeply religious Ranga.

Ooshi was awestruck by these stories. The frequency and number of his interruptions and questions were annoying. 'Appa, how do you remember so many stories?' asked young Ooshi.

'What rubbish! My memory is not so inadequate that I can hardly remember all the Upanishads and the Azhwar writings! Remember that all our great *shastras* (scriptures) have come to us through word of mouth. The mark of a true mind is the ability to learn and memorize many, many things. That is the true sign of a genius among Brahmins! But let me finish the story of Vellore, do not interrupt me,' said Ranga.

The last anecdote related by his father was about the uprising at Vellore. This town lay north of Vilakkudi. The story goes that the English, who were by now well established in Madras, had admonished the Indian soldiers for continuing to wear their caste marks. To Ranga, this seemed ridiculous. How could the personal caste mark interfere with a person's soldierly duties? Ranga pondered deeply on what his reaction would be if he were prevented from wearing his *kudumi* (tuft of hair) or his *panirandu thiruman* (twelve caste marks on the body). It seemed to be the height of unreasonableness on the part of the *vellai karan*.

Apparently that was what happened at Vellore. Hindus were prohibited from wearing their caste marks on their forehead and Muslims were compelled to shave their beards and trim their moustaches. This resulted in great unrest. Two young men, one a Hindu and another Muslim, were given ninety lashes each as punishment for refusing to comply with their orders. That was enough to set the emotions of others on fire. 'How foolish could these English be?' rued Ranga.

According to the story his father had told him with disgust mixed with awe, almost twenty people were convicted to die, some by bullets while others were hanged to death. To think of the episode even now, after almost half a century, made Ranga very, very angry.

There was, however, a positive end to this story of the Vellore uprising. From faraway England, the senior authorities had apparently instructed the less cultured local *vellai karan* to modify the rules in this regard.

'These are insensitive rules, and totally unnecessary,' the *dorai* (boss) seems to have told the local chieftains. In the impressionable mind of Ranga, in some small way, this put the English in good light. Respect for caste marks was wholly to be applauded, especially if it was coming from a strange *vellai karan*.

By this time, the father and son had covered more than half the distance. Their entry to Mannargudi would be from the *kizhaku* (eastern) side in perhaps *mukkaal mani* (three-quarters of an hour). 'So let me tell you a bit about Mannargudi,' said Ranga to an eager Ooshi.

If Vilakkudi-Rayanallur had three thousand people as per the *vellai karan's* calculation of 1851, then Mannargudi had at least ten times as many people. 'Mannargudi is huge, though not as huge as Madras up in the north,' said Ranga.

It has a very significant temple, an old one, the Raja Gopalaswami temple. The *panguni uttiram* festival at this temple was as well conducted as it was in Nagapattinam. It was said that all desires were fulfilled by a visit to this famous temple. The intricate architecture of this temple was truly breathtaking. 'I will take you there on this visit,' said Ranga to Ooshi.

'Oh, by the way, they started a reputed, lower secondary school here twelve years ago. It is called the Findlay School and was started by the Christian people who were called Wesleyan Mission,' explained Ranga to a curious Ooshi, who wondered aloud what they taught in a school like that.

Ooshi's curiosity to know more about the Wesleyan Mission did not meet with Ranga's approval. Ranga was conservative and did not quite approve of the growing influence of the Christian missionaries in the whole area. In fact, Ranga's father had told him how the Christians had even tried to convert the Tanjore Maratha ruler. The catastrophe was averted by the joint effort of a bunch of crafty court Brahmins. He wondered why Christians came to India to convert Hindus, as no conversion was possible in Hinduism—or construed as necessary.

Ooshi's curiosity was cut short with a reference to more traditional matters. 'Mannargudi was originally one big *agraharam*, filled with Brahmins like us. The *agraharam* is supposed to date back to the times of Raja Raja Cholan, some five or six hundred years ago,' explained Ranga.

'And by the way, if you have the energy to walk a distance similar to the distance we have covered, I can show you Thiruvarur. Shall I tell you about Thiruvarur?' asked Ranga. '*Appa, shollikite pongolen* (keep talking), please tell me more, it all sounds so exciting,' chimed the excited Ooshi.

'Well, you know those *Telengu kirtanais* (Telugu kirtanas) that we sing at the temple? Many of them were composed by the great saint and musician Tyagaraja, who used to live in Thiruvarur. Tyagaraja died just ten years ago. He was prolific in his compositions and passionate in his love for Sri Rama.

He composed the *pancha ratna kirtanais* (five gem songs) which are so popular,' Ranga said before breaking off to hum the songs with short pants of breath in between. He pointed out how lucky they were to be born into the crucible of music and culture.

It was a strange coincidence that the trinity of Carnatic music were all born in and around Thiruvarur—they lived contemporaneously but never seem to have met. Tyagaraja composed in Telugu.

Ranga continued his inspiring narrative, 'Muthuswami Dikshitar learnt Sanskrit and wrote in that language. He died on the very auspicious day of *Deepavali* a few years after my *upanayanam* (thread ceremony),' said Ranga with a sad note in his voice.

'And what about Syama Sastri?' egged on the young Ooshi.

'Oh yes, Syama Sastri, the oldest of them. He composed in *Telengu* (Telugu) and Sanskrit. It is sheer coincidence that he died in the same year as Tyagaraja. Our whole area is musically rich, very rich and this tradition has influenced all of us who are born and raised here. We lost these great musicians who were outstanding *bhaktas* (devotees) of the Lord in a very short time. There were special prayers at the Sri Kasturi Ranga temple in our village. This is one reason I feel good about being the priest at this temple. Son, these people were titans. My father once narrated how Syama Sastri was challenged to a music competition by another musician, Kesavayya. Syama Sastri went to the temple and prayed to Goddess Parvati to give him strength. Lo and behold, he was inspired to compose

Devi Brova Samayam Idey as an invocation to Goddess Parvati to help him. He won the competition against Kesavayya by a handsome margin,' said Ranga.

Once more, he started humming the song he had just drawn attention to. Ooshi's admiration for his father's knowledge and memory grew, as indeed his knowledge of local matters of importance.

The conversation was interrupted as the roads became more crowded; they had reached Mannargudi. It was time to find a resting place at the Brahmin *agraharam*, eat something and then set about their chores for the next few days. Ranga felt he could also attempt to understand better what was going on in faraway Delhi.

Father and son had spent some very satisfying time together.

Battle at Delhi

Eight-year-old Ooshi had never been to Mannargudi. He was completely awestruck. What a town! There seemed to be people milling about everywhere. What a difference between this market town and his village Vilakkudi! Little Ooshi was amazed.

But to Ranga, Mannargudi did not seem normal. He had been visiting this town all his life, but on this occasion people seemed to be nervously huddling in groups; almost everybody seemed to have a story to tell. Several people appeared anxious if not downright scared about the goings-on in faraway Delhi.

Several merchants and pilgrims had returned to Mannargudi from other markets and pilgrimage towns. Wherever they went they met travellers from other parts of the country. The number of stories about the goings-on in the northern parts of the country multiplied rapidly. People had hair-raising stories to tell. It seemed as if nobody in Mannargudi was transacting business. Everybody seemed to want to listen to the tales brought back by the travellers.

There was no concept of a newspaper, so who knew what was right or wrong or exaggerated? How could anyone tell?

However, every tale was discussed with so much passion and authority that it convinced Ranga and the curious Ooshi as being authentic. Ranga and Ooshi listened wide-eyed and attentive to all these stories for it was important for them to listen and remember. Or how else could they inform other villagers about these matters?

Around the month of *panguni* (March), in a northern city called Mhow, a *chekliyar* (cobbler) had insulted a Brahmin. The cause of the insult was a suggestion to the Brahmin that he allow the *chekliyar* the use of his water pot. The Brahmin was livid at this brazen suggestion, which was tantamount to defilement. At this stage, the *chekliyar* taunted the Brahmin by telling him what was happening up north with the upper caste soldiers. 'The upper castes have already been defiled,' the *chekliyar* told the Brahmin.

The *vellai karan* was compelling all the Indian soldiers to use a new kind of cartridge brought from England. This cartridge had to be bitten off by the soldier to unseal it. No dissonance so far. The problem was that the cartridges were reported to be greased with cow and pig fat.

The Hindu and Muslim soldiers were equally upset by this revelation. So indeed was Ranga! How could the *vellai karan* do this? Ranga recalled a story he had heard in his childhood about the incident at Vellore many, many years ago when Hindus were prevented from wearing their caste mark. Had the white man not learnt any lesson?

The Hindus felt that the white man was insulting them by asking them to bite into cow fat, a defilement of their religion. The Muslims were offended by having to bite into pig lard, a taboo to them. Word spread around the army towns like wildfire.

All the month of *vaikasi* (June), the rumour had people seething all over the north. The English summoned a conclave of the princes from several states to explain their proposal and seek their cooperation in persuading the soldiers to accept the proposal. It seemed that the invitees included the Peshwas from several Maratha kingdoms like Gwalior, Baroda and Indore, the Maharaja of Puri and the Raja of Banapur.

Every ruler who attended the conclave opposed the idea, deeming it misplaced and incendiary. The Raja of Banapur pointed out that Hindus and Muslims had coexisted happily for centuries. They might have fought over territory but never over religion. The English had to learn from these facts and give up their draconian proposal. But, as the raconteur narrated, the *vellai karan* was intolerant and refused to listen.

Has it not happened throughout history that when *durbuddhi* (misguidedness) enters an administration, disaster follows? '*Vinaasha kale vipireetha buddhi* (bad times follow an aberrant mind),' the raconteur said, using a locally popular phrase. He then paused to gauge the reaction of his audience.

'*Shumma kadaiye sholunge?* (Tell us what happened after that?)' the crowd egged him on expectantly.

After having tried in vain to persuade the soldiers, the *vellai karan* issued final instructions: religion-based issues were not to be raised while implementing orders issued by the army. All Indian soldiers were expected to perform their duties using the new cartridge. This order was issued just before the break of *aani* (mid-June).

The Indian soldiers immediately demonstrated their outrage. At a village called Barrackpore near Calcutta, Mangal Pandey openly defied the order. Everybody listening to this story in Mannargudi cheered. At a town called Meerut near Delhi, the soldiers rebelled. Word spread like wildfire across many army towns in the north.

Ranga was anguished to hear this story and wondered whether the narrator's quivering voice had just a touch of exaggeration. He moved on to another group to check out if such a fantastic story could really be true.

The next narrator had an even more gruesome story to tell about a small town called Bithur near Kanpur. Ranga was not sure whether little Ooshi's ears were ready for such stories. But he could do nothing; Ooshi was curious, the storytellers many.

'So what happened at Bithur?' enquired the agitated listeners in the crowd. Apparently, some white women and children had been captured by the Peshwa Nana Sahib's men near Allahabad and detained at a prison in Bithur. Every morning they were taken under armed escort to the banks of the Ganga for their ablutions and bathing. One English woman wrote a note in English, and left it at a prearranged place under a stone on the river bank. She had bribed a cleaning woman with two gold coins, begging her to carry the note to the sahibs at Allahabad. It was a great plan.

However, a soldier saw the cleaning woman pick up the paper near the river bank. She was accosted and taken to

Nana Sahib and after being whipped, confessed the whole plot. The white woman who wrote the letter was also produced before Nana Sahib. A translator was engaged to explain the contents of the note exhorting the British to attack Bithur and Kanpur immediately as the security situation was presumed to be temporarily lax.

'There you are,' argued Nana's soldiers, 'we all know that women are a nasty and tricky lot. Here is further evidence. Nana Sahib, please allow us to kill all these English women and children.' Nana Sahib held them back, ruling that it was unethical to kill women, though he finally agreed to punish the white woman who had written the note.

The soldiers went to the prison. Unable to control their anger, they killed every white person, woman or child. 'This is a hideous crime against women by Hindus,' intoned the storyteller at Mannargudi, 'and it will remain a blot on our foreheads for a long time.' Ranga agreed, his spirits sinking further after listening to this story.

Ranga and Ooshi moved on to another crowd where a storyteller claiming to know what happened in Delhi was holding forth. The fighting in Delhi was the most intense. It seems that the soldiers and citizens of Delhi had approached the virtually defunct Mughal emperor, Bahadur Shah Zafar, to accept the leadership of the forces; his only virtue being that he was the least unacceptable leader.

'How can that solution work? A leader has to lead, especially in a time of crisis. When society chooses the least unacceptable person as a leader, the outcome cannot be good. Even a simple villager like me knows this,' mused Ranga.

It was a profound thought, born out of the simplicity of his thinking. Its validity, however, had been tested by history and would continue to be so in the future.

Humble and quite aware of his limitations, the Mughal emperor accepted the titular position of the head of the Indian forces. The soldiers then went into the palace prisons and massacred about fifty English prisoners. Mayhem followed all over Delhi. The storyteller confessed that he had no words to describe the aftermath.

Ranga dragged Ooshi along, absorbing several other narratives before engaging in the business that brought him to Mannargudi. This included a trip to the famous Raja Gopalaswamy temple, a visit to the market to sell some paddy and to the office of the tehsildar to complete the documentation of his agricultural land. On the third day, it was time to return home.

Ranga, torn between agitation and the need to share all this information with his fellow villagers, rushed back to Vilakkudi. Tucked away in his village, Ranga felt he had been living in a cocooned world without any knowledge about what was going on elsewhere. However, it was his duty to call a meeting of the village elders, brief them and contemplate on the implications of these developments for their families. After all, as the temple priest, he was perceived by the villagers as being *sarva jnani* (of all-pervasive wisdom).

Famine around the Rice Bowl

Several years passed, Ranganathan and Ranganayaki had now found a suitable match for their sixteen-year-old son, now formally referred to by all as Ooshi.

Ooshi had grown to be taller than his father—fully deserving of the sobriquet he had acquired 'Ooshi'—thin as a needle. He was talkative and outgoing, a characteristic he would impart to some successors in the family.

The coy, eleven-year-old Lakshmi, Ooshi's child bride, was from a fine family in a neighbouring village. Her parents were devout. The family was not rich but the father had enough wealth to spend the money required to celebrate the marriage. Since the marriage expenses were borne by the girl's father, the financial capability of the family had to be assessed early in the matchmaking process. The girl looked strong and perhaps she could bear healthy grandchildren for Ranga and his wife. Above all, more than one astrologer had pronounced the alliance as truly blessed.

Brahmin families encouraged child marriage, unlike some other castes where families tended to marry a tad later. If a family had to go far from the village to find a match for their daughter, it was viewed with suspicion. Was there something wrong with the girl? Was there a defect in her horoscope? What would people say? So, as soon as possible, the girl's parents would start the search for an able and competent son-in-law, who would promise the girl to 'grow old with him', as per the Vedic injunction during the marriage ceremony.

Ranganathan and Ranganayaki led their lives as 'God had ordained'. They were firm believers in the theory of *karma*. Their life in the village was extremely busy, what with farming for three crops—*kuruvai, samba* and *thaladi*—cash realization, raising the kids, buying a few ornaments for the women, and above all, performing their *vaidika karyam* (religious work) to the satisfaction of the community. Money was not plentiful, but the family managed to subsist off their humble earnings.

After Lakshmi attained puberty, she came to live with Ooshi. Two sons were born soon after, as per the norm in those days. The older was named Ranganathan Junior in keeping with the tradition of naming the eldest child after the grandfather. The younger son was Krishnan.

When Ooshi was twenty-seven, in 1876, Lakshmi bore him a round-faced, roly-poly boy. They called him Gopalan. Ooshi's three sons, along with their sisters, grew up in Vilakkudi, during the 1880s and 1890s.

I am Gopalan's grandson. Gopalan was a brilliant student of both the Sanskrit Vedas and the Tamil *Divya Prabandam* written by the Azhwars. It was common among Brahmins to have a working knowledge, if not mastery, of both. As a result, my grandfather earned a sort of graduate degree called UVe, which stood for *Ubhaya Vedanta*.

In his later years, he was addressed by the venerable title: *Ganapadi Ooshi Sri Ubhaya Vedanta Gopalachariar Swamin of Vilakkudi*!

I was most impressed to hear the title when I visited the village many decades later and was introduced as the grandson of this august gentleman. He bequeathed my father several books of high learning. My father enjoyed reading them; my generation regrettably lacked aptitude, and so lost the knowledge.

The family elders progressively concerned themselves with the tumultuous pace of social change. Like their ancestors, they had managed to lead their own lives reasonably well, but how would, for example, little Gopalan cope with the inexorable pace of change all around?

What constitutes a tumultuous change is a matter of individual and relative perception. Events experienced emotionally and impacting the life of a person are usually considered tumultuous. Changes that were impacting the lives of the village folk like Ooshi in Vilakkudi were, therefore, perceived as tumultuous.

The first big change was the effect of the Great Madras Famine of 1877. Ooshi perceived the fall-out of the famine very clearly because it had the incidental benefit of earning a small fortune for him. He recalled the episode narrated below with great emotion as Gopalan had also been born around the same time.

For decades, whenever the Cauvery flooded, water would cover the whole Tanjore delta area which included Vilakkudi. The area was thus immune to variations in monsoon, making it exceedingly fertile.

The problem began with a very unfavourable weather pattern in 1877, disturbing the entire Deccan. In fact, this problem affected other parts of the country as well. The rest of the country, however, was not blessed with water supply as the Tanjore delta area. With no meteorological department to depend on, watching for signals of an approaching monsoon was the main occupation of farmers across the country.

Ooshi, living in Vilakkudi, thus became an indirect beneficiary of this imbalance. Paddy prices shot up due to the shortage all over the country. As the tehsildar said, Tanjore became the granary of the Deccan. The prices realized by Ooshi were unprecedented and in a few years, the family was transformed from being poor to being quite well-off. Money ceased to be a day-to-day concern.

Although the family had earned quite a bit, word in the village was that it was a disaster elsewhere. *Oru kodi* (ten million) deaths had occurred all over the country according to the Mannargudi gossip. Most disturbingly, the rumour was that the cause of these deaths was the sheer incompetence of a *vellai karan dorai* called Lord Lytton, the principal officer stationed in Calcutta.

What pained Ooshi the most was the scandalously expensive public function organized in Delhi to mark Queen Victoria's coronation in England as the Empress of India, while the common people reeled under the effects of the famine.

Ooshi felt strongly that what the people wanted was not a queen, but some rice!

At Mannargudi, raconteurs estimated the unprecedented scale of the Delhi extravaganza. The numbers were mind-boggling—beyond Ooshi's comprehension. The function, to which sixty thousand English guests were invited, lasted a week. That translated into enough food to feed twenty Vilakkudis for a whole week! The quantity of grains and vegetables were quickly estimated by a mathematically adept Ooshi after factoring in that the *vellai karan* ate a lot more food than the Indian. He was appalled; was all this information true?

A few years later, he heard that the political implications of the famine were so major for the English that a party called the Indian National Congress (INC) had been formed. Strange new things were happening in the world around Ooshi, and this was the second change he had noticed.

The idea for the INC was born in 1885 in Madras when seventeen people assembled as members of the Theosophical Society. Formed by Helena Blavatsky and Henry Olcott in 1875, the Society's aim was to engage in an intellectual enquiry into the spiritual traditions around the world. Then, as now, India soon appeared on their agenda as a subject for better understanding. They made Madras their world headquarters. Political awareness suddenly seemed to increase.

The purpose of the Indian National Congress was to 'obtain a greater share in the government for educated Indians and to provide a platform for civic and political dialogue of Indians with the British'. Through the Theosophical Society, the INC attracted prominent Indians like Womesh Chandra Bonnerjee, Dadabhoy Naoroji, Dinshaw Vachcha and Romesh Chander Dutt. In later years, the INC made the Great Madras Famine the cornerstone of their critique of the government.

The third change Ooshi witnessed was related to transportation. A monstrous, puffing steam engine train, moving a large number of people, faster and more effortlessly than Ooshi had ever experienced in his lifetime. Ooshi had never boarded a train, but he had viewed Tiruvarur station from outside. The reports were that the train journey from Tiruvarur to Madras could be completed within a day.

The story about the advent of the train from Chintadripet to Red Hills in Madras had trickled into the village many years earlier. A rail line had been laid to haul quarried stones back and forth. But soon after beginning operations, the company running the train service was reported to have closed down. Later, around the middle of the 1880s, railway lines were laid between Nagapattinam and Tanjore via Mannargudi. These trains could carry passengers.

This meant that Gopalan could go to Tiruvarur and get a train all the way to the big city of Madras. In fact, there were reports that Bombay and Calcutta had been connected, a bit like a blessed marriage between a boy and a girl. By interconnecting two different railway companies, it was possible to complete the whole journey of two thousand miles between Bombay and Calcutta by train. The ageing Ooshi and the young Gopalan pondered over the consequences of this development for a Brahmin family.

How would they observe their *acharam* under such circumstances? How would they perform the injunctions of ablution and *sandhya puja*? It was mindboggling.

The fourth big change that swept the countryside was the advent of the newspaper. The villagers were aware that an English newspaper called *The Spectator* was being published once every three days in Madras for several years now. Since it was in English, the contents were unintelligible to the villagers; it was obviously meant only for the *vellai karan*. In all probability, the news had something to do with the departure and arrival of ships at Madras, the price of food and cash commodities, the availability of imported clothing for the foreigners, the sort of stuff that most Indians would have little interest in—at least in Vilakkudi.

One of the features of this paper, recounted in later years, was that it carried advertisements for the England-made soaps—Sunlight, Lifebuoy and Pears. The English makers of these soaps adopted an imaginative ploy to promote these products. They printed calendars with the pictures of goddesses like Lakshmi and Saraswati. Rural Indians loved to collect pictures of gods and goddesses; they would frame these pictures and mount them in their prayer rooms.

My interest in such minutiae was heightened by the fact that they became lessons in rural marketing later in my career. When I joined Hindustan Lever in 1967, I became the brand manager for Lifebuoy and Pears. By a neat twist of coincidence, my daughter became the Social Mission Manager for Lifebuoy in 2010! Her husband was the officer responsible for Pears.

But to turn back the pages of history once again, about the time Gopalan was born, a Tamil newspaper called *Swadesamitran* was being published from Madras. It was started by G. Subramanya Iyer 'to create awareness about economic backwardness of the Indians and the alleged discrimination by the British'. The firebrand poet, Subramania Bharati, became its editor between 1904 and 1906, stirring up revolutionary ideas amongst the readers of the *Swadesamitran*. As kids growing up in Calcutta in the 1950s, we often heard our mother reciting his poem:

Senthamizh Naadenra Podinele
Inba theyn vandu paayidu kaadinele
Yengal thandair Naadenra Pechinele
Oru Shakti pirakkadu moochinele

[*The mere mention of our ancestral land*
is honey to our ears and
we are energized by a new spirit
by listening to stories about our ancestors.]

In no small way have I felt inspired to write this book for this very reason.

Gopalan would read a copy of the newspaper, which began to be available around Vilakkudi as he grew to be an adult. This gave him valuable information about current affairs, not just in and around Madras, but even in other parts of the country.

The fifth change concerned written communications. In 1879, a rectangular postcard of thick paper was introduced by the authorities. Very affordable, it cost a quarter of an *anna* (one sixteenth of a rupee). The postcard could be delivered to any address in the country. It was the cheapest form of communication and represented the first 'bottom of the pyramid' innovation as future management gurus would term it.

The use of the postcard required the writer to be literate. Unfortunately, this excluded most people in Vilakkudi, indeed in most other parts of the country. Therefore, the educated people, mostly Brahmins, developed new occupations of 'letter writers' and 'letter readers'.

These new activities added to the income stream of the Brahmin family, apart from increasing their already exalted positions within society. For a small fee, they would write whatever news the villagers wished to convey to their friends and relatives. The practice was to deliver as much information as the postcard could hold. A fine handwriting of small but legible letters fetched a premium.

All these events were beyond the comprehension of both the ageing Ooshi and the young Gopalan. Viewed concurrently, these events were perceived as big sociological changes. All that Gopalan was told as he approached adulthood was Ooshi's view that 'it would be difficult for Gopalan to manage his life in the manner that Ooshi had led his own life'.

'Well, God takes care of all,' Ranganathan and Ranganayaki rationalized. 'A good soul never loses faith in the Lord. That is why the *vaishnavite* believes so strongly in *sharanagati* (complete surrender to the Lord),' they reminded themselves.

As the subsequent narrative will reveal, each generation was apprehensive about the next generation's ability to cope with change. But, in its turn, each generation coped marvellously. Therefore, the family fared well.

Obscure Controversy

As Ooshi aged gracefully into retirement, Gopalan and his two elder brothers, Ranganathan and Krishnan, grew up to be strapping young adults. In particular, all three of them demonstrated great diligence in chanting the Sanskrit Vedas as well as the Tamil Azhwar writings. Gopalan in particular, had a deep, sonorous voice making him a welcome candidate for temple functions where a *parayanam* (chorus/recitation of sacred texts) was conducted.

During his adolescent years in the 1890s, Gopalan attended a discussion at the local temple about a hundred-year-old controversy in the Kancheepuram temple between two sects of his community, the Iyengar Brahmins.

Initially, Gopalan could not fathom what the controversy was all about. From what little he could glean, it seemed to be an extremely inward-looking controversy. With all the changes in transportation and communication, he wondered whether this controversy displayed an attitude of living too much in the past among some of his religious compatriots.

Traditions and religion are useful, but should they become a divisive dogma? He pondered upon this question in silence and mused: over several millennia, Hinduism has been known for its tolerance and respect for other religious creeds.

He ferreted out the facts, which were incredibly complex and legalistic. Here is what he figured out:

Among the Brahmins of Madras, there were those who worshipped *Shiva* (called *Iyers*) and those who worshipped *Vishnu* (called *Iyengars*). Not surprisingly, each group perceived themselves as superior to the other. The Iyers outnumbered the Iyengars by a factor of four, thus making the Iyengars a miniscule community at the very outset. An additional conflict served to vivisect the Iyengars further.

Saint Ramanuja, the acknowledged patron saint of all the Iyengars, lived eight hundred years earlier, around 1000 CE. Four hundred years after Saint Ramanuja, two great savants expounded slightly differing liturgies and temple procedures, which appealed to two different groups of devotees. One sect favoured the classical Sanskrit Vedas, while the other championed the Tamil Azhwars, who used the peoples' language.

This difference is similar to the split between the Christians. Catholic liturgy was compulsorily in Latin until the twentieth century, while the Protestant liturgy had switched to local languages. For example, in British India, the Protestant liturgy was in Hindi and Tamil to make it more accessible to the people.

The first group of Iyengars favoured Sanskrit as the language of prayer. Their savant had designed a number of verses for temple worship. The followers specialized in learning the Vedas in Sanskrit. They came to acquire the title of 'vadagalai', meaning those from the north of the Tamil country. The vadagalais used a caste mark of U on their forehead. (I happen to be a vadagalai!)

Another group followed the second savant who had also composed verses, but in Tamil. They were based on the writings of the Azhwars, who lived between the sixth and the eleventh centuries. They came to be referred to as the 'thenkalais', meaning those from the south of the Tamil country. They wore a caste mark which resembled a Y.

In short, by the fifteenth century, the U and Y categories had developed within the already miniscule Iyengar-Brahmin community. Both categories accepted the Vedas and the Azhwars, but while the Us ascribed a superior status to the Vedas, the Ys deemed the status of the Azhwars higher.

To a modern mind, this would appear like splitting hairs, but to those devotees it seemed to matter a lot!

In his manual of Chingleput District during the nineteenth century, an Englishman, C.S. Crole, observed the difference: 'The vadagalais are more straight-laced in doctrine and place more reliance on forms and rituals than the thenkalais... The vadagalais will not read sacred books or chant verses except in Sanskrit, while the thenkalais, while revering Sanskrit, use Tamil also.'

The Devaraja Swamy temple in Kanchipuram is a famous vaishnava temple, revered for its historic and religious importance. It has the status of being one of the three most holy vaishanava places of worship. It was in this hallowed temple that a major controversy broke out between the two sects around the late 1790s.

The issue was whether the temple markings (on the walls as well as the ever-so-visible temple elephant) and the language of liturgy should be in the U method or in the Y method! Each sect claimed its method as being the original one adopted in the temple, particularly after a major temple restoration in 1711.

The dispute was referred to the district authorities and courts over the many years that followed. Two things were striking in the denouement of events. Firstly, that the judicial and administrative systems seem to have been fully preoccupied with this matter compared to other important issues; secondly, the pronouncements of English judges or administrators were subsequently quoted by both parties, even though it was far too traditional a matter to be adjudicated by foreigners.

Around 1800, when the thenkalai procedures were claimed to be practised in the temple, some vadagalais were alleged to have 'mischievously and unilaterally changed the procedure'. Mr Hodgson (1799) and Mr Greenway (1801) imposed a fine on some vadagalais while deciding this matter.

But in 1894, when Gopalan heard the story, the temple elephant had just died. The death of the elephant revived old wounds, he learnt.

Apparently, when the elephant died in 1894, the Us donated a new elephant with a prominent U mark. The Ys promptly objected. In reality, as events unfolded, it was unclear whether the temple owned any elephant at all between 1894 and 1942!

The controversy was, most likely, deliberately kept hanging in various courts and departments, a practice that subsequently became the norm of civil litigation in independent India. In this way, the authorities avoided any movement or decision in a sensitive matter.

But then again in 1942, the Maharaja of Travancore presented the temple with an elephant that bore a U mark. All hell broke loose. This case must be the longest pending unresolved legal dispute in India!

Gopalan wondered whether this was what religion and temples were all about. He was somewhat modern in his thinking by Vilakkudi standards and felt that such frivolous matters should not engage the community, the administration or the judiciary. However, the matter was well beyond his ability to resolve or get involved with. Further, it did not suit his stern and austere personality to engage in what he privately thought was a fruitless debate.

Rising Challenge of Caste

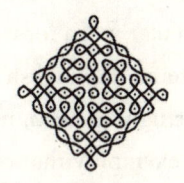

Gopalan was not wholly in sympathy with his fellow vadagalais's excessively traditional approach; he also realized that the family had to adapt to the tremendous changes that were going on all around. As many writers who wrote autobiographies in that era would indicate, village life was beginning to change in myriad and significant ways.

In his memoirs, *Hand of Destiny*, C. Subramaniam (an architect of India's green revolution in later years), described village life in his native Pollachi as, 'Our family was the premier family in the village. The patriarch of the family was my grandfather, Perianna Gounder. The village consisted of families belonging to various castes. There were carpenters, blacksmiths, potters, washer-men and barbers. These [sic] formed the second rung of the society. At the lowest rung came the untouchables. They lived in a separate portion of the village.'

K.P.S. Menon, a Foreign Service officer of free India, wrote in his autobiography *Many Worlds*: 'Moreover, through no fault of theirs, the Brahmin boys in our school were not particularly liked by the others. They had prodigious memories;

they scored high marks in all subjects and especially in Mathematics.'

The word 'caste' in Indian society has very complex connotations. The vernacular word for it is really *varna* (colour). As a word, caste had entered the English lexicon from sixteenth-century Spanish and Portuguese *casta*, meaning lineage, race or breed. I mention this to exemplify that caste has had a meaning in every society for many centuries. It is not an exclusively Indian evolution, unknown elsewhere. No doubt the Hindu version can be regarded as distinctive and rigid compared to other societies, but more of this in the last chapter.

In the 1850s, Travancore state had about twenty-five thousand Tamil Brahmins, just one per cent of the population. With English education becoming widely available after the 1860s, many of the Tamil Brahmins added to their academic qualifications. The Maharaja's College of Trivandrum, then affiliated to Madras University, began turning out graduates in the 1870s, mostly Tamil Brahmins. In 1880, besides the Dewan, three of the four Dewan Peshkars were Brahmins. They also accounted for a majority of the district and high court judgeships, as well as the licensed lawyers and pleaders.

Around 1900, although the Brahmins accounted for only three per cent of the population of undivided Madras Presidency in British India, well over two-thirds of the graduates of Madras University were Brahmins. The coveted professions of education, law, judiciary, science, medicine, administration and politics were dominated by Brahmins.

Chakravarti Rajagopalachari, Alladi Krishnaswami Iyer, Sir C.V. Raman, Sir C.P. Ramaswami Iyer, Rt. Hon'ble Srinivasa Sastry and the mathematical wizard, Srinivasa Ramanujan, were all doyens of this community, dominating their fields in the first half of the twentieth century.

This position was not unique to Madras Presidency. Such a high-profile minority group anywhere soon falls into bad ways, or attracts envy, or both.

The clarion call against this Brahmin dominance came from E.V. Ramaswami Naicker, who was popularly known as *Periyar* (The Elder). He was the son of a wholesale merchant who had started life as an assistant to a stone mason. Periyar was born in 1879, which made him a contemporary of Gopalan. At the age of twelve, Periyar joined his father's business and showed great promise in its management.

Until he was thirty, he strengthened his father's business in Erode. He was appointed the Secretary, and later President of the *Devasthanam* (local temple) Committee. By 1920, he had held several positions of public importance. Between 1919 and 1924, Periyar was an active Congressman.

By the 1920s, Periyar's exasperation of Brahmin domination in the Congress was gradually increasing. The last straw was an incident in the Tirunelveli district.

A residential school in Cheranmadevi, partly funded by the Indian National Congress, was run by V.V.S. Iyer, an active Brahmin Congressman. In 1925, Periyar received a complaint that Brahmin and non-Brahmin children were not only served different meals but were also fed separately. Periyar advised Iyer to treat all children similarly to avoid instilling caste hatred in them. Iyer ignored the suggestion, much to the annoyance of Periyar.

Despite his close association with Rajaji, Periyar quit the Congress at the Kanchipuram conference of 1925. He started his *Suya Mariyadai Iyakkam* (Self-Respect Movement), and later joined the Justice Party, largely comprised of non-Brahmins. Just as the French revolutionary Rousseau worked hard to arouse the self-respect of the French people in 1815, Periyar emerged as a sort of Rousseau of Tamil Nadu.

In the first Self-Respect Conference held at Chingleput in 1929, two resolutions were adopted: the first, that caste should not be a distinguishing factor among human beings, which meant that wearing of caste marks or using one's caste in the name should be stopped; and second, that people should stop supporting temple rituals and not build new temples.

Periyar spearheaded his tirade through the Justice Party into a fairly wide movement. Being cast in the role of an iconoclast, he stood for anything that was anti-Brahmin. Religion and rituals were scoffed at. Gods were taboo and common sensibilities were numbed with public acts of burning icons or defiling temples. He began his discourses with the incantation:

There is no God, there is no God.
There is no God at all.

He who invented God is a fool.
He who propagates God is a scoundrel.
He who worships God is a barbarian.

His attempt was to isolate the three per cent of Brahmins by classifying them as Aryans, that is, northerners in origin, whereas the ninety-seven per cent of non-Brahmins were depicted as Dravidian in origin. As later events would show, there was lack of logic in depicting a general category of non-Brahmins as a homogenous group. In the process, Periyar perpetuated an acute caste distinction between and among the majority of non-Brahmins. The landless Harijans were tempted to convert to Islam and Christianity.

Today, the Brahmins are a hopeless minority in Tamil Nadu. But were the Brahmins the problem? Probably not, because communal and caste conflicts are as acute as ever.

For instance, a conflict in 1948 at Ramanathapuram took five days to subside; the 1989 Bodi conflict took twenty-three days to calm down; and in 1995, there was devastating caste violence between the Thevars and the Devendra Kula Vellalars in the southern districts of Tamil Nadu, the situation taking much longer to normalize. The progressive increase in the duration of violence is the result of the resistance offered by the Devendra Kulu Vellalars to the caste practices of the Thevars.

It is interesting to note that in 1997, the Dravida Munnetra Kazahagam held a three-day convention at Salem. The DMK Chief, M. Karunanidhi, lamented that the ideals which had inspired the birth of the Dravidian movement were now facing destruction. Even though egalitarianism was certainly an article of faith for Periyar, this was conveniently jettisoned by the DMK over the years. In constructing a Tamil identity, the DMK left the unequal ownership pattern of land out of its agenda. This was hurtful to the dalits, who came to occupy positions in the administration and demand a role in the political discourse. The intermediate castes, the same sections that constituted the muscle of the DMK's political campaign, would not concede this, and in this lay the seeds of further strife.

Even today, almost one hundred years after the beginning of the Dravidian movement, the dalits of the Tamil country express unhappiness about the inequality of their social status compared to the rest of the non-Brahmins, the creamy layer of society. A few years ago, the government of Tamil Nadu released a report that showed that there was much discrimination against the dalits, but of a more subtle nature. During their study, the researchers found that 160 out of the 221 village panchayats had evidenced cases of dalit discrimination.

Generally speaking, the Brahmin was fair in complexion whereas the non-Brahmin had the archetypal dark skin. The Brahmin was proficient in Sanskrit. Tamil is a truly ancient language, in fact, much older than Sanskrit. The chaste Tamil, completely devoid of Sanskrit influence, used by Periyar and his protégé C.N. Annadurai for their effective political demagoguery was, in fact, popularized to make precisely this distinction between the Brahmin's Sanskrit-influenced Tamil and the native Tamil.

The non-Brahmin movement developed a mythology of its own, identifying the Brahmins with Aryans and the non-Brahmins with Dravidians. This powerful combination of language, flowery prose and a sing-song intonation became the vehicles on which the successor organizations of the Justice Party, i.e., DK (Dravida Kazhagam) and DMK (Dravida Munnetra Kazhagam) would build strong political, anti-Brahmin lobbies in every remote village of the Tamil lands. By the early thirties, the denigration of the Brahmins had acquired sufficient momentum to earn them the derogatory epithet, *Paapan*.

In the 1990s, a body called TAMBRAS (Tamil Nadu Brahmins' Association) started gathering momentum. Their main mandate was to secure rights for Brahmins from the ruling non-Brahmins! They wanted an economic criterion so that the impoverished Brahmins could seek some place under the sun. M. Karunanidhi, of course, insisted that his government would ignore economic criteria, and follow only social and educational backwardness.

In every society around the world there is a cycle of ascendancy and decline of changing groups of caste. This has been pointed out by the academic David Priestland. Sometimes the sages are on top, at other times the warriors, at other times the merchant and other times, the artisanal worker. The wheel of the anti-Brahmin movement has turned full circle, all within one hundred years.

Dawn of the Twentieth Century

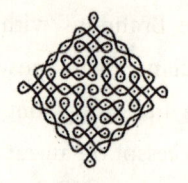

Around the year 1900, Gopalan married a comely girl, Sundaravalli, from Kombur, a small village near Needamangalam in Tanjore district. After a few years, on attaining puberty, the young bride joined her husband in Vilakkudi. Families were quite large in those days, not just in the south but all over the country—perhaps it was the desire for sons, or to compensate for infant mortality! I never ceased to wonder how such productivity and proclivity came to exist in a joint family situation, and where unremitting and sweltering heat existed almost right round the year.

Between 1900 and 1930, my grandparents produced ten children, of whom seven survived beyond the age of twenty. My father, Ramabadran (Rajam for short, meaning 'virtuous like Sri Rama'), was the second of these surviving children.

As was the practice in those days, and indeed even today, the pregnant girl would go to her parental home around the sixth month. She would return after delivery, having had some time to recoup, typically with a three-month-old child.

So it was that in June 1912, young Sundaravalli undertook the two-hour journey from Vilakkudi to Kombur. On 17 September, 1912, my father was born with the village midwife in attendance.

Like many other native practices, there appeared to be a great deal of wisdom in sending a girl away to her parental home for her confinement. Although according to Hindu marriage custom, the girl's father performs *kanya daanam* (given away his daughter), thus making the girl a member of her husband's family, parents in those days must have been just as eager to see their daughter as they are today. Girls were married young, and until they reached puberty lived with their parents—though they visited the husband's house frequently—on auspicious occasions like *Karthigai, Deepavali* and *Pongal*. In this way, attachment and love grew between the young couple.

Parents also visited, sometimes to escort the girl or to bring her back and also for inviting the son-in-law and his parents for all important functions. Therefore, the separation of the parents from the daughter in those days was more absolute compared to these days when, at least in urban India, it is quite acceptable for the girls' parents not only to visit, but also stay at the son-in-law's house. So, there seemed to be great merit in letting the wife stay with her parents on specific occasions such as pregnancy. The joint family system ensured many assigned chores for the daughter-in-law in her marital home.

In orthodox families, the daughter-in-law was welcomed into the kitchen after she'd had her *samasaranam* (formal function of initiation into the Srivaishnavite faith, somewhat like Christian baptism) and after she had learnt all the *aacharams* (orthodoxies). Likewise, she could not enter the kitchen for sixty days after childbirth; then, too, only after being administered the *panchakavyam* (a mixture of five ingredients to bring her to health). This was actually a way of assuring that the new mother had some rest, away from household duties.

Household responsibilities must have been stressful, as they inevitably are even today. So the practice of the girl going to her parents' house during pregnancy ensured her adequate rest. Typically, she would be at her parents' home for three months before delivery till three months after delivery.

Four years before my father Rajam was born, Sundaravalli had already begotten a son named Srinivasan. He was followed by a daughter who died. Sundaravalli, yearning for a daughter, found herself with another son—my father. So with her creative abilities at the fore, she saw a daughter in her second son, Rajam, ensuring it in small ways.

For instance, she affectionately called him Baby, which is used only for girls in Tamil Nadu, although boys do use this name in Kerala. She would not have his hair cut short, so by the time he was six, Rajam had long hair, which she would plait and tend with great care and affection.

Fortunately, some years later, a baby girl was born in the family. Undoubtedly, this took the burden of girlhood away from Rajam, who could now grow up normally. By this time, modern primary schools had sprung up around Vilakkudi.

Gopalan considered modern education of a minimum level essential for the next generation to cope confidently with the strong winds of change all around. So my grandfather initially arranged for my father's elementary education at Vilakkudi.

Young Rajam walked a few kilometres to school each way. He would leave home early in the morning with a lunch box containing *pazhayadu* (hand-pound, cooked rice left over from the previous night) mixed with buttermilk, salt and perhaps some spices.

This was not done to palm off the leftovers as one might assume. Such a meal was actually considered good for health. As there were no refrigerators, the rice was kept overnight in an earthen pot with a small quantity of buttermilk. As modern science might explain it, the fermentation process that occurred imbued the rice with a characteristic succulence considered easy to digest.

When Rajam returned from school in the early afternoon, he had walked a healthy five or six kilometres, played and chatted en route with his peer group for a couple of hours, tucked in a meal that was simple but nutritious. Walking under the hot sun probably made him perspire. On his return home, he would draw two brass pitcher-loads of water from the well in the backyard and give himself a good scrub down. Some ablutions, Sanskrit study and general help with the household chores would follow.

By dusk, it would be time to visit the village temple of Sri Kasturi Ranga for the evening *aarti*. After dinner under the light of a hurricane lantern with all the kids seated in a row, the bare-bodied young lads were ready for peaceful and healthy slumber, often hearing a bedtime tale from the *puranics* related by some village elder. With the cows mooing early in the morning at the *agraharam*, the young lads would once again assemble their school satchels for the day.

The school satchel itself was interesting. The first lessons in writing were with a sharp stick or the forefinger on a soft mud surface; next, the child graduated to owning a slate and a slate-stick. Not having an abacus, sea shells were used to learn arithmetic while tables were learnt by rote.

To improve the students' accuracy and speed in arithmetic, the school taught them fractional multiple tables. My father could multiply a quarter by half in a jiffy. Learning by memorizing and by word of mouth came naturally to village kids. After all, four thousand years earlier, had not the entire Vedas been passed from generation to generation by word of mouth? Once arithmetic was embedded strongly in the mind at such a young age, it conferred an amazing aptitude with numbers right through life.

Many years later, when my father Rajam worked in a foreign company at Calcutta, he would demonstrate this ability with great aplomb while his English boss would struggle with a slide rule! He related such anecdotes with great glee.

Of course, while pursuing his studies, at the age of eight or so, Rajam had his *upanayanam* (thread ceremony). The thread ceremony represented the formal entry of the child into the

Brahmacharya (the student bachelor) stage. Traditional Hindu belief recognizes four stages of life referred to as *ashramas*.

The *Brahmachari Ashram* represented the period up to young adulthood. Celibacy, study of scriptures and education were the principal responsibilities. The *Grihastha Ashram* represented the family stage—marriage, children and the ensuing responsibilities. The next stage, around the late fifties, was the *Vanaprastha Ashram*—the children would be reasonably grown up while the householder mentally prepared himself for what could be loosely termed retirement. Finally, there was *Sanyasa Ashram* by when he abandoned worldly attachments and retired for meditation and spiritual attainments.

After the *upanayanam* ceremony, the *Brahmachari* sported a *kudumi*: a long tuft of hair with the front of the head shaved clean. He would wear a white dhoti tied around the waist; he could not use the eight yard *panchakacham* as yet, a dress-style reserved for the *Grahastha* only.

In 1925, Rajam and his elder brother Srinivasan were living in Mannargudi and studying at the Findlay High School. It was the same school which Ranga had referred to disapprovingly while walking with Ooshi to Mannargudi seventy years earlier.

Quite unexpectedly, Rajam was struck by polio and confined to bed for two years. Even on resuming school, he had to seek exemption from physical training and sports. His parents, Gopalan and Sundaravalli, were alarmed and disappointed. Various herbal oils and ayurvedic remedies were tried. In later years, my father would recall one traditional treatment he was subjected to. His legs were buried knee deep in the sand on the banks of the Cauvery for several hours each day. My father's aunt (Gopalan's sister) had taken Rajam to Kumbakonam for this treatment. It is not clear what worked, but something finally did.

Because of this early ailment, Rajam was perceived as the weakling in the family. Given to being philosophical, Gopalan advised his young son to stay on in the village and look after the farm, being unable to match his brother and cousins physically.

This adversity however seemed to bring out the fighter in Rajam; he was determined to show that he was not a weakling. Gopalan had grossly underestimated the willpower and fighting spirit of young Rajam!

Against all advice, Rajam moved to Banadurai High School at Kumbakonam to make a fresh start and completed his SSLC in April 1931.

The leitmotif of converting adversity into opportunity kept recurring through Rajam's life.

The Lure of Calcutta

Although Vilakkudi was in the back of beyond, one must recognize the hyperbole in describing the rustic village scene of the early century. Change was all-pervasive, with old and familiar institutions giving way to new ones. Vilakkudi could not remain untouched.

World War I had begun many thousands of miles away, with the assassination of the Archduke of Austria in Serbia. England redeemed its promise to support Serbia, while Germany sided with Austria. The English war effort cast its shadow on India, though it was only a penumbra. Thanks to newspapers and an incident in Madras, Gopalan was able to comprehend the effects of World War I on India.

World War I manifested its presence in India primarily through the mobilization of troops and resources. However, for Gopalan, it assumed presence when the German battleship Emden, commanded by Captain Von Muller, sneaked into the Bay of Bengal on 30 August 1914, less than a month after Britain joined the war against Germany. Emden began to attack cargo ships plying between Calcutta and Colombo. In the six days between 9 and 14 September, she captured two ships and sank six others. On the night of 22 September, Emden fired 125 rounds at the giant oil storage tanks at Madras. The bombardments and the explosions terrified the population and caused a panic never before witnessed in the city.

Apparently, the episode left a lasting impression in the minds of the citizens of Madras. News travelled, even to remote Vilakkudi.

For decades after, Tamils used Emden as a bogeyman, as my mother did with us. Recalcitrant children were brought into line with the ominous warning: 'If you do not do this, beware, the Emden will come!' Emden thus entered the Tamil vocabulary with a suitable inflection, making it sound like *yumdun*.

Calcutta had been the premier commercial city of India for several decades. On 11 August 1886, *The Times of India*, Bombay, wrote: 'The position of Calcutta as the capital of the Indian Empire is a very singular one... From the sea the city cannot be attacked, as the channel of the Hooghly could be choked in half an hour; and by land any enemy must march four hundred miles through the hot flats of Bengal, only to find that his army, once arrived in Calcutta, lies under the guns of ironclads on the river. Men do not die in Calcutta but they wither. There is no scenery, nothing but dull green jungle, stretching endlessly on every side over a damp plain, on which there is not a stone, a hill, or even an undulation for hundreds of miles.'

The home of British mercantile houses, the centre of India's flourishing trade in tea, jute and coal, Calcutta had been the capital city until Lord Curzon of the Bengal-partition fame moved the administration to Delhi in 1910. Post-war activity created the demand for an expanding white-collar class to man offices in the government, ports, railways and mercantile houses. News of this opportunity in distant Calcutta reached Vilakkudi, too.

By the late twenties, the family had dispatched two of its sons to seek fortunes in Calcutta—Rajagopalan, the son of Ooshi's eldest son Ranganathan, and Srinivasan, the eldest son of Gopalan. Around the same time, families were sending their sons to Bombay, too. The logical question was: Why so far away? Why not Madras, which was comfortably closer? In the answer lies the kernel of a great social transformation that was unfolding.

Although Madras was a strong British centre, it was neither large nor growing commercially as Bombay or Calcutta. Besides, the anti-Brahmin wave had gathered firm root in Tamil Nadu already. The small Brahmin community felt threatened in a primordial fashion and it responded in an aggregate manner, with a combination of fear and flight. Earning money in far-off Calcutta was not a bad idea for a young man with a whole life ahead. However, a modernization of the classical village naming system was required if a person were to work and live away from the village.

The classical Brahmin naming system probably had its origins in the traditional Sanskrit introduction of oneself to elders. During the thread ceremony, the young *Brahmachari* is taught how to introduce himself after paying obeisance to elders.

He stoops slightly at the waist as a mark of respect and probably to get closer to the elder's ear, who is typically seated. He cups his hands over the ears to recite the *abhivadanam* (introduction). In about fifteen words recited in Sanskrit, the *abhivadanam* would explain the lineage of Rishis one was derived from—I would never have known that I hail from the lineage of three sages, Angirasa, Gargya and Shainya, had I not been taught the *abhivadanam* in 1961. Then follows the veda studied by the family—in my case, the Yajur Veda. The *gotra*, Gargya (in my case), is the next to be announced. Finally, one's own name is uttered. All this is done in the third person, perhaps as a mark of humility, and yet with the panache of an eighteenth-century ambassador presenting his credentials to a European emperor's court! An equivalent in today's modern world is a handshake with a 'Hello, I am James' introduction.

With British administration at the district level firmly established in the nineteenth century, the mammoth exercise of updating land records was in progress. Probably such an exercise required a more westernized format of name-writing. A Tamil name typically had four components: the village name, the father's name, the individual's name and the surname. My own name would read Vilakkudi Ramabadran Gopalakrishnan Iyengar. One cannot dispute its logic in revealing your identity perfectly. It is a different matter that perhaps we should not be so keen to summarily reveal who we are.

Rajam adopted the simpler G. Ramabadran, rather than the more classical Vilakkudi Gopalan Ramabadran Iyengar. The first casualty in this jawbreaker was the surname. The migrant Brahmin saw little virtue in it and dropping it would, he may have thought, help de-emphasize his Brahmin origin. Dropping the surname meant that father and son had different names. So people in the north as well as foreigners could never understand how the son of R. Subramaniam could be S. Ramadorai. Many decades later, after the Ambedkar movement for Harijans, a feeble attempt was made in the Hindu heartland to drop surnames indicating caste. The second casualty was the village name. These names were often unpronounceable to the less adept English or North Indian tongue, and at any rate, meant very little to them.

With two scions already in Calcutta, the next in line was my father. However, his polio-weakened leg prompted continual advice on the virtue of settling down to tending the fields in Vilakkudi. The young Rajam found this completely unacceptable. He, too, had to make it to the big city. But how was he to achieve his dream?

He started by demonstrating that he was no weakling. So he undertook long walks to develop his thigh and calf muscles, and over a few months, got rid of the perceptible limp completely. No village voodoo or herbal medicines; sheer willpower! Another characteristic was his exceptional gregariousness and volubility, probably inherited from his grandfather Ooshi. This quality was to stay with him all his life.

In a somewhat orthodox environment, talkativeness was easily noticed. In 1930, he learnt about a group of elderly relatives planning a pilgrimage to Varanasi and needing a young male escort. My father had recounted the long itinerary to me once. It included several major shrines—Tirupati, Tungabhadra, Pandarpur, Nashik, Tapti, Pushkaran, Brindavan, Kurukshetra, Haridwar, Rishikesh, Ayodhya and Calcutta—a considerable journey for those times.

From Kanyakumari to the Himalayas, all Hindus consider the Ganga and Varanasi extremely special. The Ganga washes away the sins of this birth and, if one is fortunate enough, be cremated on its banks in Varanasi, it is a sure road to salvation. Varanasi was visited by both Adi Sankaracharya and Ramanuja during their extensive northern sojourns. In the 1500-mile concourse of the river from Gangotri in the Himalayas to the deltas of Bengal, Varanasi is the only point where the river actually flows from south to north—an anomaly in an otherwise straight course.

I visited Varanasi for the first time in 1974 on a sales trip, flying Indian Airlines from Delhi. I visited the ghat, took a boat ride on the river and prayed at the Kashi Vishwanath temple in between my business schedule. Although I was a believer, I could not help reminding myself that these were somewhat touristic chores I was performing, almost as one might take a little time off to see Baz Bahadur's fort in Mandu or the Sun Temple at Konark.

I had not come to Varanasi on a pilgrimage, had undertaken no arduous journey to get there, and in my western-educated, city-bred mien, I could not help noticing the squalor and filth, the sheer exploitation of a blindly faithful populace. Though I forbore from the ritual of an early morning dip in the Ganges, I compromised an uneasy conscience by carrying back a small copper urn of Ganges water.

But surely it was different for the devout, elderly widows of a remote village of Tanjore planning to visit various places of pilgrimage in 1931! Apart from broadening perspectives, perhaps such trips afforded a break from the monotony of life in the village. They could hardly plan a visit to the Nilgiri Mountains, but a trip to Badrinath or Varanasi would definitely meet with social approval!

In those days, it would take almost fifty days to cover the major pilgrim centres of India. They would, of course, carry their own food rations for the entire journey, and the services of a young lad were always welcome as a male escort and for odd errands at stations. Rajam talked through his plan with the ladies' group. His ready wit and gregarious nature perhaps appealed to them; they were weary of an austere village existence.

He would perform all the duties expected of him; in return he placed two conditions. First, they would pay his third class fares and expenses (there used to be first, second, inter and finally third class in trains even when I was growing up). The second was a request that they handle the last part of their journey independently, as he wished to stay back in Calcutta. It is doubtul if they were excited by this proposition, but his winsome ways won them around.

Next, nineteen-year-old Rajam had to tackle his stern father. Gopalan was not known for any outward displays of warmth and affection. He was short in communication, spartan in his personal habits, firm in his decisions and a stickler for discipline. How did one tackle such a person? My father worked out a plan to address his father through the head of the family—Ranganathan, my grandfather's eldest brother.

A few years earlier, Rajam's older brother, Srinivasan, wanted to go to Calcutta to join his cousin who had a job in the Stanvac Oil Company. Being scared to approach his stern father, Srinivasan requested his uncle Ranganathan to intercede on his behalf. Ranganathan, moved by young Srinivasan's earnestness and determination, blessed and presented him with twenty rupees for expenses, besides persuading his younger brother, Gopalan.

Now Rajam decided to follow a similar approach.

The three brothers, Ranganathan, Krishnan and Gopalan, were now occupying separate houses, contiguous to one another and clustered around the village deity in the Kasturi Ranga temple. The construction of the houses though similar, was not identical. The division of property had resulted in Gopalan inheriting the ancestral home in which Ooshi had lived.

The front of the house presented a small awning with a raised stone platform called the *thinnai,* on either side of the entrance. This platform was the favourite perch for the head of the family to sit and relax, watch the world go by and receive visitors for a cozy, village chat. Passing through the wood-framed entrance, one stepped into a large courtyard in the centre, surrounded by corridors leading into rooms. An old and ornate teakwood swing invariably adorned the main sitting area which had direct access into the kitchen and backyard.

This traditional village design would be the inspiration for the construction of my house in Bangalore half a century later.

Having sold his services to the tourist party, Rajam ventured into his uncle's house one afternoon. The fifty-five-year-old patriarch of the family was sitting on his swing, savouring his afternoon coffee. The young lad sat at his uncle's feet, breaking into pleasant chatter. During the next hour or so, the youngster explained his plan which would lead him to his greatest wish—to strike out in Calcutta and earn money to send back home. The old Ranganathan listened carefully, his years and experience enabling him to sift the blindness of youth from earnest commitment.

By dusk, the patriarch had conveyed his whole-hearted approval of the plan. Handing over a gift of a hundred rupees (a princely sum in those days), he spoke with great affection, or with clairvoyance (possibly both), 'Rajam my boy, I have no doubt that you will be successful in Calcutta, but I also bless you to earn more than any of our boys. I shall speak to your father tonight.'

Rajam was delirious with joy. He fell at his uncle's feet in the customary four-time obeisance, stated his *abhivadanam* and slept under the starry July sky, spinning out his dreams for the future.

This particular incident holds a great deal of significance for me. Fifty-four years later, in 1984, I happened to visit Vilakkudi—my last visit having been thirty years earlier.

I was in my late thirties, on a valedictory visit to the vanaspati factory of Hindustan Lever at Tiruchirappalli before relinquishing charge as general manager of the foods business. After a light lunch, I set out for Vilakkudi via Thanjavur, Vaduvur and Mannargudi. My grandparents and most of their generation had passed away twenty years earlier, and with most uncles having left the village, I really had no one in particular to meet, nothing specific to accomplish. Sentiment, nostalgia and curiosity had combined to take me on this journey. By 4 p.m., I reached Vilakkudi.

The village looked very different from my recollections as a nine-year-old boy. The village post office looked quite large, there seemed to be many more shops and, above all, there was electricity. As I stepped out of the car, I was surrounded by local kids and adults, offering to help me find whoever I was looking for. After some enquiries, I found my way to the *agraharam*. As the car came to a halt, time seemed to stop.

Here was a picture unchanged; I had stepped back in time, reliving the memories of a nine-year-old in 1954.

The road was still untarred. The houses were just the same. I recognized the houses of my granduncles, Ranganathan and Krishnan. But Gopalan's house, alas, had ceased to exist. Instead, there stood a two-storied, multicoloured, modern structure built and occupied by Pakkirsami Pillai's family. Pakkirsami Pillai was a wealthy landlord. Clearly, it indicated changing times; he was a non-Brahmin living within the *agraharam*, and in my view, a welcome change.

Of course, things have changed even more since my visit to the village in 1984. I remember an article I had read in *India Today* about Tirunageswaram in Tanjore district. For decades, twenty-five Brahmin families lived on Sivan Sannidhi Street. While bare-chested Brahmins sporting the sacred thread could be seen on the front verandahs of the houses, women in nine-yard sarees would flit in and out. During the 1970s and 1980s, ten of the twenty-five houses were sold by the Brahmins to Muslim families. The others changed hands with Pillais and other communities. Basically, the Brahmins, erstwhile landowners, progressively found agriculture less remunerative, and therefore sold and migrated from the village. This metamorphosis, not surprisingly, had reached Vilakkudi also.

As I looked around, a bent old widow emerged from her home. Peering at me, she asked who I was looking for. 'Oh, nobody in particular. Just looking around,' I replied. Suddenly, with a remarkable feat of memory, she exclaimed, '*Unnam illadai inga yaaru varuvaa?'* (Who would come here to do nothing?) You look like Rajam's son. He had the same look and gait. You cannot be any other. Are you not Rajam's son?'

I must confess I was completely unprepared for this. I said yes, even while I held back from asking who she was. Would it display poor manners or lack of deference? In a trice, she summoned a passing kid, asking him to fetch Sampath, the surviving son of Ranganathan. I was now the cynosure of all eyes and the sole charge of Sampath, who introduced all those around—cousins, uncles and aunts.

The village priest was pulled out of his home and the gates of the old Kasturi Ranga temple opened up for a special prayer. As I stood there watching the *aarti*, I was reminded that in this same temple over the last century, my great-great grandfather, great-grandfather, grandfather and father had all prayed.

The benedictions and blessings of this village deity were no doubt, very special and I felt privileged to be the recipient on this occasion. The chanting of the prayers resounded in the cavernous walls of the temple, letting my imagination fly. My forefathers seemed to be speaking to me through those mute walls with a benign smile, welcoming me home!

After the visit to the temple, I was taken by Sampath to his house. Being the youngest son of Ranganathan, the patriarch, he now lived in that very house. He ushered me into his house and seated me on the same swing from which, fifty-four years earlier, my father had received the blessings of Ranganathan.

He narrated the story with great skill and sentiment and concluded, 'Now that you are seated on the same swing, you can realize how accurate his prediction was. Amongst all the cousins who left this village for Calcutta, Rajam has been quite successful. He has earned well and supported his less fortunate relatives periodically. Earning money and being successful are all relative.'

At the end of each day, one needs to be thankful for every mercy and good wishes from every benefactor. And who can be greater benefactors than one's forefathers? Every person leaves unalloyed benediction and the purest of love for the next generation. I felt privileged to savour a bit of this universal truth through a personal experience.

And so it was that by *Dussehra* of 1931, Rajam found himself in Calcutta under the common roof with his brother, Srinivasan and his cousin, Rajagopalan. He was all of eighteen, ready to face the bustling metropolis of Calcutta!

The Great Metropolis

Rajam was wide-eyed as he assimilated the journey from the railway station at Howrah to his brother's residence at Kalighat. There was a bridge on the Hooghly River, a predecessor of the bridge that we see today.

He passed through Prinsep Ghat, Kidderpore, Alipore, Hazra Road, Kalighat and finally reached the house at Pratapaditya Road. Named after Pratapaditya Roy, a seventeenth-century Hindu king of Jessore, this road commemorates the king's act of valour when he declared independence from the reigning Mughal emperor.

Over the next several days, Rajam walked around Calcutta, a city whose size he could never have imagined. Everything seemed to have a story around it. There were many unusual if not abnormal sights. As he would realize in his later years, the unusual or abnormal was normal in Calcutta. Rajam absorbed these stories with the enthusiasm of a nineteen-year-old village bumpkin.

The city was founded by Job Charnock in 1690 at Sutanati. Charnock was reputed to have been a dashing officer. The story goes that when he saw a widow about to commit *sati* (self-immolation), he prevented her from doing so and married her. This created three scandals simultaneously: the bypassing of *sati*, widow remarriage and an Indian girl marrying a foreigner!

From there the city grew. Calcutta was either loved or dreaded by the English. In 1863, Sir George Trevelyan wrote, 'Find, if you can, a more uninviting spot than Calcutta... it unites every condition of a perfectly unhealthy situation.' Charles Stewart wrote, 'Should the English ever be driven from all parts of India, the English could find an asylum in Bengal where no enemy would venture to follow.' Later, Rudyard Kipling wrote essays on Calcutta titled *The City of Dreadful Nights*.

Rajam found that apart from the native Bengalis, there were migrants from everywhere in the city. Many strange languages were spoken: English (of which he had rudimentary knowledge), Bengali, Hindi and his native language by an emergent Tamil community near the lakes in southern Calcutta.

He was confused by the Bengali habits. There seemed to be a Bengali way of sitting, with the left leg drawn up and the left hand dangling lazily upon the left knee. The right leg was then made to shake. This was in stark contrast to his accustomed posture of sitting with both legs folded in a stance of discipline.

He found that many people had a name that ended with 'jee' like Banerjee, Mukherjee and Chatterjee. There were, he learnt, thirty ways of writing the Bengali name Chakravarthy, a common name in Madras, with spellings ranging from Chuckerbutty to Chuckervertty!

Finally, he learnt that every Bengali has two names: an elegant, Sanskrit-inspired name—for example, Ardhendu Kumar (a prince with a countenance as handsome as a half moon)—and a *daak naam* (pet name), which had no relation to the real name and was quite often, ridiculously nonsensical, for example, *Tublu, Tuktuk, Handu*.

There were, however, some similarities between the Tamils and the Bengalis as observed by Rajam. The Bengalis observed *Poila Boishakh* (New Year) on more or less the same date that the Tamils observed their *Varusha Purappu*. They also seemed to prize education as Calcutta University was already reputed to be the 'highest degree granting factory' in the whole country. The annual Durga Puja festival displayed idols shaped in nearby Kumartoli. The atmosphere of pageantry and gaiety reminded him of the *panguni uttiram* temple festivals in his native Tanjore and the decoration and display of dolls during the annual *navaratri* festivals at home.

In 1879, P.W. Fleury and Company demonstrated the use of electricity and its potential value to the metropolis for the first time. Thirteen years later, in 1902, the city got its first electric tramcar. In 1905, Lord Curzon announced his highly controversial plan to partition Bengal into Hindu and Muslim areas. Even the Nobel Prize winning Rabindranath Tagore expressed his strong disapproval of the partition as indeed King George V had done in England.

In 1912, coincidentally on April Fool's Day, another blow was dealt to Calcutta by the Governor General. He announced a plan to shift the capital of the British Empire to Delhi. This was opposed by many, including the English head of one of the biggest mercantile firms, who wrote in *The Englishman*, 'We have spent a great deal of money in recent years building up Calcutta.' Over the next many decades, Calcutta would be hollowed out of its super-active mercantile vigour for a variety of reasons.

During the 1800s, Dwarakanath Tagore had founded the first managing agency in partnership with the English, named Carr Tagore Company. Later, Tagore started the Bengal Coal Company and the Union Bank. Under a fabled neem tree in New China Bazaar Street, an equities stock exchange had started operating.

In the early part of the twentieth century, Bengali entrepreneurs had started manufacturing and marketing of products, led by the Bengal Chemicals and Pharmaceutical Company (medicines and consumer products), F.N. Gooptu and Company (pens, pencils and accessories) and the Lily Biscuit Company. Those were times when industry was perceived as an adventure. The examples of success from Bombay like Jamsetji Tata, Ardeshir and Pirojsha Godrej, and the Gujarati textile magnates provided inspiration to the Bengali entrepreneurs. Calcutta, it appeared to Rajam, was a vigorous mercantile city.

Of course, mercantile activity was dominated by the British business houses. As Rajam walked awestruck around China

Bazaar Street, Royal Exchange Place and Fairlie Place, he noticed many British-sounding firms like Martin Burn, Andrew Yule, Imperial Tobacco and Mackinnon Mackenzie. His companion and guide told him the amazing story of James Lyle. Lyle was an ordinary person who had shot to stardom and wealth. He had reached the highest echelons of Mackinnon Mackenzie. Rajam was inspired. Clearly this was a city with opportunities for those willing to work hard, Rajam surmised.

The most unusual street, according to Rajam, was Chitpur Road. Reputed to be Calcutta's oldest road (probably four hundred years old), it ran vertically from the south to the north of the city. People engaged in varying trades all along the road. The *murgihat* (chicken market), Jorasanko (twin bridges over a creek), *kasais* (butchers) all appeared almost sequentially along Chitpur Road. A part of Lower Chitpur Road was reported to rival Chandni Chowk of Delhi as an interesting market place.

Chitpur Road also housed the aristocracy. Tagore Castle and Ghosh Mansions in Pathuriaghata were prominent with a hoary history. Another impressive and classical structure was Mullick House built by a wealthy aristocrat called Jadulal Mullick.

Rajam just could not fathom two aspects of life in Calcutta: first, unlike his native place where the wealthy appeared austere, why did these Bengali aristocrats display such extravagance? Second, how could Chitpur Road simultaneously accommodate the extremely wealthy and extremely poor? This anomaly of Calcutta still intrigues many.

Finally, the burning question that remained in young Rajam's mind was how could a traditional village lad with a tuft of hair, no education beyond school, no knowledge of languages other than Tamil and a modest amount of English, make good in this frenetic metropolis?

Emergence of the Professional

Rajam's career was a roller-coaster ride. This story is about his career. A surrogate peek into someone else's career story affords a lot of practical learning.

Rajam decided to become a stenographer, an occupation that few know today. Stenographers were in demand among the mercantile offices in Calcutta. All his acquaintances enrolled to take stenography lessons, so did Rajam.

The initial years in Calcutta posed many challenges. Rajam attended tutorial classes in spoken English and practised speaking English in front of the mirror until English became his language of communication. On the other hand, his Hindi and Bengali were interspersed with generous doses of Tamil even after many years. Calcutta and its work environment brought forth unfamiliar challenges; Rajam had to contend with strange food and patterns of dress. But he adapted quickly, learning from his experiences every day.

After learning stenography, he secured a job in an office with a salary of thirty rupees per month. This allowed him to become a contributor to the family rather than remain a dependent. He recalled later that it served to boost his self-esteem and confidence. It also encouraged him to think independently about what would be good for his career.

Soon he made an iconoclastic resolve. He decided that he would change his hairstyle from the traditional tonsure and pigtail to the normal city haircut. For the traditionals in those days, this was tantamount to revolt, totally against social sanction. To his relatives and parents in the village, this was a sign of the rapid deterioration in his standards. Others read it as the first sign of the distinctive character of this boy.

For an extrovert, sitting at an office for several hours was boring. After a few years, he made his second iconoclastic decision—to quit his job. Those were days when no middle-class lad ever quit a job! Fate was kind—he landed a job in the sales department of a tobacco company called Carreras, a predecessor of today's Imperial Tobacco Company (ITC Ltd.).

His job was to sell cigarettes in Orissa and Andhra. This act of quitting a safe and steady job for an unknown occupation was further evidence to the family that the lad was set on a risky path—'a Brahmin boy selling cigarettes, *aiyyayo*!' At this rate, they would soon smell strange odours from his breath!

Cigarette-selling built supreme self-confidence in Rajam. He met people from diverse professions—distributors, retailers, competitors' salesmen, company managers and many more. As a newcomer, he performed some tasks on his own. However, for other jobs, he had to rely on others like the distributor or the clearing agent or his coworkers. He began to learn that getting work done through others is at the heart of a manager's job.

Rajam travelled widely, observing customs and beliefs which were quite different to those he had learnt at home. He had to discuss and solve transactional business issues such as orders, payments, logistics and merchandising. While travelling, he also got to observe his bosses at close quarters, their ingenuity and their frailties and, in general, the fickleness of human nature. Such travel and field-selling brought with it the uncertainties and insecurities of field work, but he would not trade them for the more comfortable atmosphere of a staid office in Calcutta.

After a few years, Rajam decided it was time to return to Calcutta. With a contemporary hairstyle and the confident gait of a successful and ambitious salesman, Rajam came back to do something different, though unsure of what it would entail.

A career evolves in strange and unplanned ways. When you are young, you are prone to believing that you can plan your career. But sometimes, influences may deflect you into unplanned pathways, the consequences of which you appreciate much later.

Rajam met a friend, who advised him to become a GDA, as it would offer great opportunities to earn money steadily. Accepting this positive influence, he enrolled for the Government Diploma in Accountancy, a predecessor of the Indian Chartered Accountancy qualification. This encounter with an unnamed, older friend had set Rajam on a completely different course.

A foreign insurance company announced a vacancy in its accounts department. Rajam decided to apply.

His ready wit and grasp of numbers endeared him to the foreign bosses. He began a steep climb up the organization. He became a member of gentleman clubs like Calcutta Club and Ordnance Club. Soon, he could hold his drink at a party and enjoy the company of those who attended the mercantile socials that were common in the Calcutta of those days. The very middle-class Rajam was on the way to becoming part of the upper echelons of Calcutta.

Rajam always had great empathy for the less privileged. He treated them with compassion and alleviated their problems whenever he could. It is possible that his early physical difficulties nurtured this sense in him. His sense of compassion manifested itself in his response to the terrible Bengal famine of 1943. Another manifestation of this empathy was in his readiness to help needy relatives. Rajam was forever grateful to his uncle for encouraging him to leave the village and also for parting with the huge sum of a hundred rupees as a blessing. His uncle had said, 'I pray that you earn many times this amount during your career. Use part of that money to support your relatives, some of whom will be less fortunate than yourself.'

Rajam took the advice seriously; he would often recount his uncle's advice and how he implicitly accepted the responsibility of educating some of his nephews, and bearing the marriage expenses of some of his nieces. Like his brothers, he shared the accident of his prosperity with indigent and needy relatives throughout his life.

When India became independent in 1947, Rajam got an unexpected break. Many foreigners left the country and consequently, top-level vacancies within companies were now available to Indians. Rajam was lucky to have joined a foreign insurance company where he had established a good reputation. As a result, he was appointed Chief Accountant and Company Secretary, one of the three top posts held by Indians in the company. His salary was 1500 rupees per month, a very high salary in the early 1950s. He had truly arrived!

It is axiomatic that precisely when you attain success, the seeds of your weakness begin to sprout. Strength begins to manifest itself as a weakness. And when strength becomes a weakness, it traps the individual. I call this a bonsai trap because the person does not realize that the strength has become a weakness. Typically, the weakness surfaces as a dilemma or a problem needing a solution.

The other two top posts in Rajam's company were held by fellow Indians. Both were sons of wealthy professionals from Madras. In fact, both had been to England for higher studies, were eminently qualified and had the right background in the perception of the European bosses. While in his own judgment, Rajam felt equal to the other two, he was unhappy that others did not view him in the same light. He wondered whether the lack of western-style education and his village roots were the reasons.

It was never clear to my young mind whether there was a problem or whether Rajam simply believed that there was a problem. By the middle of the 1950s, he had worked himself into a frenzy; he convinced himself that he was not being accorded his due by his employer—be it salary, respect or status. His agitation was not about how he was treated by his employer, but the inferior treatment meted out to him.

This feeling of unhappiness, because of the perception that someone else is being treated better, is so common in management careers. It is surprising how self-destructing the responses of managers can be when they try to remedy such perceived unfair treatment. Every manager has experienced this at some stage of his career.

Rajam discussed his predicament with close friends. He also talked over the matter with my mother, Rukmini, who had uncanny common sense. Rukmini advised him to be patient and not to disturb the equilibrium of relationships. She felt that with six kids to be raised, family life needed to be undisturbed. His friends gave him similar advice. But Rajam remained restless.

He felt that as he was only in his mid-forties, he could seek a fairer future for himself rather than accept an injustice. At work, his questioning of how things were done was increasingly perceived as the sign of an indifferent team player. His iconoclastic nature and extroverted, gregarious personality, which had served him well all these years, now played to his disadvantage.

Soon, he resigned from the company with the supreme confidence that many would be waiting to offer him a top job immediately. He felt righteous about the act of resigning, almost triumphant. The subsequent developments posed many difficulties for him.

No acceptable full-time job materialized for four years because the salary, the city of posting or the image of the job appeared inappropriate to him. Potential employers seemed to note that he was not even a graduate. Rajam had never imagined that this would be a disqualification, considering he had over twenty years of work experience. The lack of a college degree had not obstructed his career path in the insurance company, where he had joined at the bottom and worked his way up. Sure, there were some offers, but with a lower salary, or diminished status or at an inconvenient location.

With a large family to support, he had to dip into his savings. Not having the benefit of higher education himself, he would not consider compromising the quality or the extent of expenditure on the education and upbringing of his children. There was nothing to economise on except for minor domestic expenses, a few parties or movies.

The very attribute that made him a leader for almost twenty years—self-esteem—now took a beating, bruising his ego and pricking his pride. Painfully, and consistently, Rajam's effervescence was eroded as he approached the age of fifty.

Then the penny dropped; he fought, and with renewed energy and vigour. His insight was elementary: when you are in trouble, just focus on getting out of trouble. Do not worry about getting out with elegance.

The fighter in him stood him in good stead as he suffered through four years of uncertainty. Get a job, and don't worry about what others think. Sure enough, he landed a job in faraway Bombay on a salary that was lower than what he had earned four years ago, and the prospect of living in a small two-bedroom flat instead of a palatial home with a garden.

The fighter in Rajam surfaced again. He renewed himself during the last ten years of his professional career—in a different industry, in a different city and with a different lifestyle, but with great personal learning and professional satisfaction. At the time of his retirement he was the head of purchasing in a multinational company; contented, professionally and personally.

Rajam was a learner at every stage of his life and career. He always liked to recall that he was a middle-class person, and like all middle-class people, he learnt more from his failures than from his successes.

Raising a Family

While the previous chapter was about Rajam's professional life, this one is about his personal life.

My father used to tell us that he started his professional life on a salary of thirty rupees per month. In the fifties and sixties, we could not imagine how this could possibly be true. My father was meticulous about keeping a record of his expenses. So, notwithstanding our disbelief, there was definite documentary evidence. The method followed was that every earning member would hand over his salary to the head of the joint family. The wife of the family head would cook and take care of the household. As younger members got married in the village and returned to Calcutta with their brides, the senior lady would play a supervisory role in inducting the new bride and in assigning her a role in the running of the household.

My father got married in 1935, the alliance being fixed in the traditional way. Elders would carry a mental roster of eligible boys and girls in the community. Connections would be established through this network. The *gotra* had to be different because a boy and girl of the same *gotra* were deemed to be sister and brother, descendants of a common patriarch some several centuries ago! The difference in age could be up to ten years, and the families considered had to be compatible in status, customs and values. There was no question of a marriage without exploring horoscopes.

But why was there a need for a horoscope? And who would make it?

In those days of absence of birth registry, the equivalent of a birth certificate was the horoscope. As soon as a child was born, the family elders would hasten to have the horoscope cast by the village astrologer. All he needed to be told was the place, date and time of birth. A piece of paper with two adjacent square boxes showing the position of various planets would be drawn up. For the rest of his life, this horoscope would be seen and interpreted by various astrologers as and when the concerned person desired such an interpretation. Whom should he marry, would he have children, would he get a much sought after promotion or raise, would he keep good health? The range of questions about one's future is understandably endless; what is amazing is that the range of answers is equally endless!

When I became the CEO of Brooke Bond Lipton in 1995, an astrologer cast the horoscope of my company, based on the fact that the company was registered at Calcutta on 12 September 1912 at 11 a.m. Armed with this information, he made several forward-looking statements to me which fell outside the purview of any regulator!

In 1936, a son was born to my father, but the child died young. In 1937, a daughter, Jaya, was born. She was a bright-eyed, lovely child and as later years would prove, a particularly talented girl. Her early education was at Kalakshetra, which was run by Rukmini Devi Arundale, the gifted dancer. Jaya must have imbibed the atmosphere of culture in Kalakshetra, and with the talent inherent in her genes, she blossomed into an outstanding exponent of vocal Carnatic music in later years. She is the only one in my nuclear family to show competitive, professional talent in the fine arts.

Unfortunately, Jaya's mother kept poor health. I do not know what her ailment was, suffice to say she had consistent health issues. She stayed back in the village and father would see her only during his biannual visits to the village. She died a few years later.

Whatever her ailment may have been, she had borne him a lovely daughter. Father was, till his very end, eternally grateful for this gift. He spoke about Jaya's mother only occasionally, but always in positive terms. For the next forty-five years of his life, he dutifully performed her *aapthikam* (annual rite) when the spirit of the departed soul is believed to return for a temporary tête-à-tête with those remaining. His devotion and sense of duty to her made a deep impression on my young mind.

On 12 July 1941, Rajam's second wedding took place. Rukmini was the daughter of a small-town lawyer, Karur Soundara Rajan. As the name suggests, the family originated from Karur near Coimbatore. Soundara Rajan set up his practice in a small village called Gobichettipalayam, about 120 kilometres from Coimbatore. He was a thespian who took great delight in theatre and acting in plays. His legal practice must have been modest because the family was not very comfortable financially. No sooner than Rukmini reached the age of eighteen, the family started to look for a suitable alliance.

My mother was exceptionally beautiful, fair with light brown eyes. There is adequate photographic evidence from her younger days to testify to her dazzling beauty. She had been trained in Carnatic music, as all young girls in middle-class Brahmin households were. Why would the parents of a pretty, eighteen-year-old girl consider an alliance as the second wife of somebody?

My mother recalled the positive impression created by my father. His genial and jovial nature as well as his unfettered willingness to discuss his predicament openly had a positive impact on my mother's family. It may have helped that my mother's mother was a second wife to my grandfather, whose first wife had died early. Anyway, the handsome salary of my father, his amicable nature, the social pressures of an adolescent and unmarried daughter at home—all these factors obviously converged in the elders solemnizing the alliance.

Given the prevailing standards of behaviour, my father displayed great brashness in writing letters to my mother after the parents had agreed to the alliance. For several years thereafter, my maternal uncle would recall mischievously the scandal created by my father's letters to my mother in Gobichettipalayam village!

As was the practice, the newly wedded couple moved into the joint family, which comprised some cousins and an elder brother, all with families. I never understood how they all managed to live together in just eight hundred square feet of living space. Several years later, I saw the flat where the joint family had lived at 2, Pratapaditya Road in Kalighat. The flat was on the fourth floor with no elevator. Living together in a joint family and pooling the earnings into a common fund must have generated great difficulties for the individual members. However, the sheer discipline of following the accepted social norm resulted in lowering the costs of living and using the meager savings to send money back to the village.

In this way, Srinivasan and Rajam managed to finance, in part, several obligations—the wedding expenses of three sisters, the medical expenses of one sister who was spastic and the educational expenses of two younger brothers. Srinivasan and Rajam came through to everybody as people with a missionary sense of duty to family, great concern at the human level for every member of the rapidly expanding family and a willingness to stretch themselves to help with some exigency or the other in the village.

Rukmini and Rajam had quick successes with their children: the birth of a son, Raghavan, exactly ten months after marriage, and a daughter, Saroja, a year thereafter. Over the years, I observed my father as a man of speedy decision and swift action. Clearly, he demonstrated both these qualities in the way he added to the family.

My brother, Raghavan, was named after his great-grandfather, Ooshi Veera Raghavan, as was the tradition. This way, a few names were repeated every second and third generation. Raghavan was born a tall kid and my mother often recalled how the old aunts used to measure the child with a string to admire his length as he lay in his crib.

Indeed, Raghavan grew up to be thin as a reed at six feet and two inches, and until his mid-thirties, could easily qualify for the nom de plume, Ooshi. Thanks to modern diet and more sedentary work environments, Raghavan in later years put on weight, although not disproportionate to his height. This earned him the humorous sobriquet of *Gundu Ooshi*. There was a pun on the word *gundu*. In common parlance it means a pin with a head, the kind that is used to hold papers together; *Gundu* also means fat!

My sister, Saroja, born soon after my brother, was left in Gobichettipalayam with our grandmother. Till the age of three or so, she had free run as the only available grandchild. Her reputation was of a forceful and aggressive little girl, who got what she wanted by any means possible; in her later years, she grew up to be the most docile and accommodating person in the family. Raghavan, on the other hand, was a very docile child when young, evoking everybody's compassion for his helplessness. In his adolescent years, he became quite forceful and aggressive. My mother always marveled at the ways of the Gods for this transformation in her two first-borns. It was unimaginable for her to accept a docile son and an aggressive daughter!

Between 1937 and 1944, the joint family was very busy. Srinivasan and his wife had a daughter and a son, while my father had three children—Jaya, Raghavan and Saroja.

Srinivasan was working with Reckitt and Colman and my father had joined Hercules Insurance Company, a general insurance company. Thus, both had good jobs in prestigious British firms, but the political environment was very volatile, a world war was on and each morning must have brought forth new uncertainties that could interfere with their dreams for the future.

Until the turn of the century, India had been exporting nearly ten million tons of food grains. This had transformed into imports of a couple of million tons of food grains, thanks to population increase. Of course, it is a fact that Bengal experienced a poor harvest in 1941. Several districts saw protests. While the British authorities chose to downplay the shortages, the situation was serious—severe shortfalls and no imports. Mahatma Gandhi wrote in his *Swaraj,* 'There are no imports of food and cloth from outside of our country, and the scarcity can only worsen as the war develops.'

The Indian point of view was that the primary cause of the famine in the 1940s was the extent to which Churchill and his advisors chose to use India's resources in conducting the war against Germany. The acts of the British in their self-interest resulted in scarcity of food and sky-rocketing prices in India. As war signals were building up in Britain, Churchill recruited a highly trusted physicist, Professor Frederick Alexander Lindemann, in London. Lindemann's job was to help the government take scientific decisions with respect to food supplies, cross-national shipping and stockpiling. The bureaucrats in London soon realized that the professor's hold over the

Prime Minister was far in excess of theirs. 'No one fought harder to keep up the war-time ration of food for the British people,' reported one official. The influence of the professor on Churchill was surprising to the English bureaucrats as no two people could be further apart in their habits. Churchill loved cigars and multicourse meals with whisky, while the professor was a teetotaler, vegetarian and a non-smoker!

The Statesman published reports about the famine, and editorials blamed the government for spreading a famine. One report stated that a baby was trying to drink milk from a dead mother's breast. Another report by a well-off college student said, 'When sitting down to eat at home, we would close the windows. The plaintive cries from outside for food were too difficult to listen to.' Another report said that if a baby was seen abandoned on the pavement, nobody picked it up lest they got involved in a police case.

That it was a terrible famine is well recorded in history books, and yet the western countries were asking India to tighten her belt. In his speech, the Indian Agent General to Washington, Sir Girija Shankar Bajpai, responded poignantly. He addressed the Combined Food Board: 'In the south and west of India, one hundred and twenty million people are within uneasy hearing of the fluttering of the wings of the Angel of Death. The Bengal famine has taken an unimaginable toll of death. We seek only bread and we seek it only to live. For us, there can be no tightening of belts, because you cannot any further straighten an already straight line.'

The famine affected my father a great deal. He was thirty-one and energetic, and rightly felt that he ought to help the famine relief effort. For several months, he took active part in a famine relief kitchen near Kalighat. Later, he would recall the pathetic condition of the famine-affected, the enormous logistical obstacles in procuring and delivering the famine relief supplies to those for whom they were intended.

When he died in 1989, among the letters of condolence we received was a moving letter from one of his associates in this famine relief effort. The letter described in several lucid paragraphs the nature of the endeavour, the scope and scale of the relief effort and the sterling role played by my father. I was moved to tears as I read this letter sitting by the body of my dead father.

I had kept the letter aside with the pious intent of responding to the author of the letter. In the days following, I could not find the letter and thus lost a paper containing an intimate and first-hand account of my father's role in the famine relief kitchen at Kalighat.

I learnt of another episode, this one about the matchless courage of my father in 1946, one year before India gained independence. At that time, Bengal was ruled by a Muslim League government, led by H.S. Suhrawardy. As a trivia, I should mention that Suhrawardy had studied in my school, St. Xavier's Calcutta, where he graduated in mathematics about fifty years before I graduated. The times were volatile and talk of partition was in the air. Unfortunately, in the East Bengal districts of Noakhali and Tipperah, Hindus had been massacred. Many writers of the time opined that it was no ordinary civil riot but a pre-meditated killing of Hindus by the Muslim majority. The riots and disturbance that followed cascaded into Calcutta as well.

Rajam's brother, Srinivasan, had a brother-in-law, Kuppuswamy, a young, upcoming lawyer-accountant who was apprenticed to a lawyer in a Muslim-dominated area of Calcutta. As the terrifying Noakhali riots spread to Calcutta, Kuppuswamy failed to return home one evening. Srinivasan and his wife were distraught. They could do nothing except imagine the worst that could have happened.

Being energetic and action-oriented, Rajam set out on his own, explored the Muslim area incognito, found Kuppuswamy hidden in the cellar of his Muslim boss and rescued him. Both of them ran all the way out of the dangerous area with sword-wielding crowds at their heels at various points. My uncle Srinivasan was ever so admiring of his younger brother's dare-devilry that he would narrate this story for many years to the rest of the family.

Unfortunately, death by lynching seemed to be Kuppuswamy's destiny. Twenty-five years later, as a senior officer in a jute mill, he was lynched to death by labour union leaders in Metiabruz, Calcutta. His death had nothing to do with his actions except that he was seen by the union leaders as a representative of the management. Jyoti Basu's rabble-rousing United Front government in Bengal in the early 1970s had whipped up passion among militant labour unions.

My two older siblings, Jaya and Raghavan, were born in the south at their maternal grandmother's home in accordance with the prevailing custom. My sister, Saroja, was born in Calcutta; in fact, my mother's labour pains were rapidly followed by delivery, and she was born in the ambulance itself! I was born on Christmas Day, 1945, at Shishumangal Hospital, Lansdowne Road, Calcutta. Therefore, by birth and domicile, I was entitled to be called a Bengali as indeed my two brothers who followed, Narayanan in 1947 and Srinivasan in 1951.

By this time, the practice of attaching Calcutta to a classical South Indian name had begun, exemplified by a person who went on to become a director of the cigarette major, ITC. His name was C.R. Jagannathan, standing for Calcutta Ranganathan Jagannathan.

I suppose I should have been called 'Calcutta Ramabadran Gopalakrishnan'. But it was difficult to live life in the second half of the twentieth century with so long a name; and, in a concession to the changing times, my name was abbreviated to Ramabadran Gopalakrishnan. For the next nineteen years, I grew up in balmy Calcutta, a city of huge contrasts, but also of great warmth.

A Wonderful Childhood

Calcutta used to be the premier city of the country at the turn of the century. The Bengalis would proudly proclaim: 'What Bengal thinks today, the rest of India thinks tomorrow.' I have recollections of living in four localities—Elgin Road, Ballygunge Circular Road, Rashbehari Avenue and finally, for several years, at Hastings. Anyone familiar with the city would agree that most of these localities are not quite the heart of Bengali Calcutta. Despite this, Calcutta and Bengal had a profound and positive influence on me in my early years.

My eldest sister, Jaya, was studying at Kalakshetra in Madras. We were five kids in the house, so it was a busy household. My father had passed the GDA soon after the war. In 1949, when the Institute of Chartered Accountants was formed in India, he was admitted as an Associate of this Institute. Thus, he came to add an A.C.A. after his name.

He was completely self-made; he had not been able to study in a formal college for graduation so these three letters were very important for his visiting card.

Many middle-class Indians had started to acquire double degrees by stretching the family finances and by sheer persistence and hard work. It was, therefore, a matter of great pride to display these accoutrements. I remember that erudite people were referred to by their degrees, educational and professional accomplishments. A Mr Srinivasan and a Mr Shekhar had studied in England. Mr Ayyangar had done his BA and LLB, and was practising law. Mr Mahadevan had earned a dual degree, BSc and BE, and had joined the Indian Engineering Service. And so the list went on.

Here were the trappings of a new caste system, based on what and where one had studied.

The second dimension of this new caste system was about where you worked. If you worked in one of the old British mercantile houses of Calcutta, you had probably done quite well, but were second to the even higher ranking ICS, or its successor service, the IAS. The roster of companies that was talked about with awe was quite long—Imperial Tobacco (later ITC), Imperial Chemicals (later ICI), Lever Brothers (later H.L.L.), Metal Box, Andrew Yule, Mackinnon Mackenzie, Bird and Company and so on.

Between Dalhousie Square and Fairlie Place was the commercial area where many of these great companies of yore were situated. Friends would be referred to by their names, but often pre-fixed with their company name, to help easy identification.

So there was Tea Board Venkatachari, National Carbon Santhanam, ITC Sundararaman, Reserve Bank Ramanujam and ICI Sundara Rajan. The most memorable appellation I can recall was for one Mr Ramanujam who was the Director of the Central Potato Research Institute, Patna. He was referred to as Potato Ramanujam; I was never sure whether this was with his express agreement. In 2013, I mentioned this form of naming quite casually to a long-standing college friend, who also happens to be an Iyengar. To my great surprise, he recognized Potato Ramanujam as his sister-in-law's father-in-law! That says a lot about the size of the community and the theory of six degrees of separation.

I think this practice was unique to the Madrasis of Calcutta. And if it was, it must have been the modernized version of their traditional way of naming themselves with village, father, and caste, all strung together. The principle was the same, the components somewhat modernized! Father himself was called Hercules Ramabadran because he was the Company Secretary and Chief Financial Officer of Hercules Insurance Company. The address was 16, Hare Street. I still remember a narrow road perpendicular to the busy Strand Road running alongside the Hooghly.

One frequent visitor was Hindu Gurunathan. He was the Sports Editor, or Sports Correspondent of the Madras paper, *The Hindu* and a specialist in cricket. I remember him as a genial and warm person who could do two wonderful things for us youngsters—he could tell us first-hand stories about our cricketing idols, and occasionally take us to Eden Gardens to watch a test match. Both were greatly enjoyable.

We would hang on to his every word—what Polly Umrigar said to Pankaj Roy in the dressing room or the exploits of Nari Contractor and Subhash Gupte. The West Indies tour of 1958 had two fearsome bowlers, Roy Gilchrist and Wesley Hall. Seeing Wesley Hall stride up his twenty-three steps for the run-up before bowling filled my young heart with terror. On the other hand, there was a stylish left-handed batsman called Garfield Sobers, who went on to become one of the all-time greats of cricket. We must have asked Hindu Gurunathan too many questions or possibly requested one too many tickets; he stopped staying with us, preferring the stylish Great Eastern Hotel or Grand Hotel where the players would be put up.

Father must have been doing quite well professionally and financially. In 1954, we moved into a large bungalow at 3, Leonard Road, Hastings. This was quite close to the Hooghly River in a rather exclusive and cosmopolitan locality.

The house had seven rooms, a garden (very well used by my brothers and myself for some sort of cricket) and outhouses for servants. All the rooms had red oxide tiling and tall ceilings. The rent was 450 rupees per month. This was expensive by the standards of those days when my father's salary was perhaps 1500-2000 rupees per month. But in the eyes of the family back in the village, Rajam was doing very well indeed. About two hundred metres from our house was a maidan called the Brigade Parade Ground. Across the road from the maidan were a row of houses called Jubilee Lines, the residential quarters of army officers.

The maidan had three distinct sections in it. One section was public, where groups of kids would pitch stumps and play cricket. It was a miracle that people did not suffer serious skull injuries. Amateur bowlers hurled the red ball to unskilled, swipe-hungry batsmen. The result of the contact, if any, was more the outcome of the science of statistics than of physics!

There was a Varma family of four brothers who, along with our four brothers, contributed to some competitive cricket. Through sheer coincidence and unbeknown to the parents, fifty years later, Beru Varma's daughter Nisha and my son Anirudha met in Harvard. It was quite amusing when Anirudha hesitantly broached the subject of wanting to marry Nisha. My instant recognition of Beru Varma surprised him. It was a huge relief to Anirudha that my wife and I had no questions to ask about the family and whole-heartedly supported his choice.

The second part of the maidan was a polo ground. I think it belonged to the army. Every morning, snorting horses would arrive, ridden by smart young men in polo dress. They held a mallet-like device in one hand. With great speed, the horses and their riders would approach a hard ball which had to be directed into goals, much like hockey. I must confess that I found the game quite terrifying; it was always a wonderment to me that there was not a huge pile-up of horses and men, while the ball would be sitting some distance apart in quiet isolation and innocence.

Polo acquired a clear overtone of status when I saw Prince Phillip, Duke of Edinburgh, play a game at the Calcutta Polo ground; he had accompanied Queen Elizabeth II on one of her state visits. Queen Elizabeth's coronation took place in 1953 when she was quite young.

The third and last part of the maidan was an athletics track. I do not know if it was meant for the army, but we kids were permitted to jog on those tracks. Weekly holidays at school were on Thursday and Sunday. We brothers must have spent at least forty per cent of our holidays on these open maidans, a clean and an altogether agreeable life of fun, frolic and exercise.

Calcutta was a highly social city. The exclusive restaurants on Park Street were only to be seen by us kids, never visited. Skyroom, Magnolias, Flury's, Trincas, all together gave my young mind the feeling that Park Street could well represent the highest density of classy restaurants anywhere in the world. Walking past these and turning into Chowringhee took one past the Museum to Esplanade. Grand Hotel with its fabled Firpo's Restaurant stood en route in mute testimony to the several great historical events witnessed within these portals. An invitation for a dinner and dance at Firpo's probably represented the high point of social life in the Calcutta of the fifties.

Father used to work in Hercules Insurance Company, a part of Ralli Brothers, founded and run by a Greek family. The CEO at that time was Sir Strati Ralli. Father's office used to be at 16, Hare Street.

I recall these minutiae fondly. Many decades later, I chaired a successor company called Rallis India Limited, which had been taken into the Tata fold. During my chairmanship, I visited the Calcutta office. Lo and behold, the Rallis India office was still at 16, Hare Street. I walked around the floor to the cabin where my father sat. I even managed to procure for my archives a statement of accounts for 1947 and 1948, both signed by my father in his capacity as Chief Accountant. I was emotional and nostalgic.

The other delightful gadget of the past was the radio. Remember that television was completely unknown in the India of the 1950s and 1960s. There was a humongous valve radio in the drawing room which would take five painful minutes to warm up. Those interested had to go to the radio and switch it on well in time to listen to the news.

In the late 1950s, we heard of a radio based on transistors, which meant that the radio could move around with you rather than you having to go to the radio. Father brought one in 1960, to our great excitement, when he went on a business trip abroad.

Father used to entertain occasionally at home. Some of them were black-tie dinners, especially when there were European visitors. Among some of the names I can remember were foreigners called Mr Weingartner, Mr Euthomopolous and Mr Chronopolous. Painfully, we learnt that the last 's' was not to be pronounced! After the guests settled down with a drink, father would call us out to be introduced.

My elder brother Raghavan's task was to crack a joke from his ever-increasing compilation; Srinivasan's (the youngest) task was to play the mouth organ which he had acquired on one of his birthdays. My sister Saroja, brother Narayanan and I were in between, and could not quite rustle up any special role, other than wear our best clothes and smile politely. After the mandatory half hour was over, we would retire to our homework and sleep, while the elders would enjoy an evening of mirth and conversation.

A potentially traumatic incident occurred in Ooty during a family holiday in 1948. I was only two years old, so I have no firsthand memory of the incident. But the effects of the incident were all pleasant and the whole family remembers it fondly to this day.

Our family included my parents and five kids with ages between thirteen and three at the time of the incident. My youngest brother, Srinivasan, was yet to be born. There was a Punjabi family also from Calcutta holidaying in Ooty. The Sahgal family coincidentally had five children ranging in ages from twelve to one. The two families were, in a sense, matched in numbers and age profile. They, however, did not know each other.

On a sunny day in 1948, the two families went boating in the Ooty Lake, which was quite clean and inviting in those days. Ooty being a hill station, the water was quite cold and the picnickers were well wrapped in woollens. The two families were in adjacent boats. Seated at the edge of the boat were the elder girls of the two families, Jaya in ours and Prabha in the other. Each was tending to the youngest of the family, Narayanan in our case, and Bittu in theirs.

The families egged on the fathers to have a friendly race. In the excitement of a feigned race, the occupants of the boat would gesticulate and cheer. Sometime during this process, entirely by accident, Prabha dropped the five-month-old Bittu into the water.

Confusion ensued. The father, Lal Chand Sahgal, jumped into the icy water to rescue his last born. I am not sure if it was because of inadequate swimming skills, the icy water or simply fear, but Lal Chand struggled in the water. My father decided not to jump in because as there were two people now in need of help. He steered our boat towards the family, drew up alongside, and helped the father and the child out of the water. They were both shivering. He took off his coat to cover them and managed to pull the boats to the shore where there were many to assist.

This incident brought the two families together to become lifelong friends. I recall attending Prabha's wedding to a handsome merchant navy officer, Dev Katiyal, around 1955, my first experience of a Punjabi wedding—quite 'undisciplined and riotous' compared to the sober Tamil wedding of my sister, Jaya, in 1954.

The years went by, but the families kept in touch. Bittu Sahgal went on to become a national icon as an environmentalist, promoting tiger conservation. When I joined Hindustan Lever, *pitaji* and *biji,* as I used to address Lal Chand Sahgal and his wife, generously asked me to stay with them. I did so for several months until I moved out to another place.

They were warm, generous and initiated me to the 'strange' ways of the Punjabi. They ate dal instead of sambhar. They ate chapattis for good health and rice when unwell, exactly the opposite of the practice in my Tamil home. I learnt to adapt.

In fact, I adapted so well that *biji* proposed to find me a Punjabi wife. My mother strongly disagreed and quietly accelerated her hunt to find me a suitable Tamil Iyengar bride!

Episodes that Touched Me

I have noticed that even siblings brought up together in the same house and circumstances have somewhat differing memories of their childhood. The difference is not in the narrative as a whole, but in the detail of recall, and the episodes recalled.

In this chapter, I narrate some episodes that I found fascinating, and that have stayed with me. I owe my memory of these tales to my father's outgoing personality; he used to tell us stories with great excitement and gusto.

The first and most dramatic event related to my parents' residence at 9 Elgin Road around 1950. For those who know Calcutta, Elgin Road and Woodburn Park are adjacent and are considered fine localities. In fact, Woodburn Park had the South Club, famous for tennis. As kids, we joined the Bengal Lawn Tennis Association's coaching scheme at this club.

Elgin Road and Woodburn Park were also the localities where two well-known personalities lived—the leader Subhas Chandra Bose, later famous as Netaji, and his elder brother Sarat Chandra Bose. The Netaji Research Bureau is housed in one of these buildings. As we played hopscotch on Elgin

Road and Woodburn Park, the buildings would be pointed out and their history related. Children love stories and I still remember what we were told.

Subhas's ancestral home was a three-storied building built by his father at 38/2 Elgin Road, a short distance away from 9 Elgin Road, where we lived in 1950. The fact that Subhas stayed there, and that it was from this house that he made his dramatic escape in 1940, fascinated us. For us, the year of his escape was a part of recent history—a mere ten years ago.

Subhas went to school at Cuttack, in Orissa, at the famous Ravenshaw College, which I visited many years later. He studied at the prestigious Presidency College in Calcutta and, later, at Cambridge. He passed the Indian Civil Service examination.

Several developments caused Subhas to feel disillusioned; he was very distressed at the state of affairs in the country. There exists a relatively unknown letter, archived at the Netaji Research Bureau, which has been quoted by his grand-nephew, historian Sugata Bose. In 1913, this is what Netaji wrote to his elder brother, Sarat Bose:

My dear brother,

Another year has rolled by and we find ourselves responsible to God for the progress or otherwise that we have made during the last twelve months.

When I survey my last year's work, I cannot help reflecting on the goal of life. Tennyson I think is an optimist and thinks that the world is progressing day by day. Is it really so? Are we really nearing our longed-for goal? Is our dear country on the high road to progress? I can't think so. May be good may come out of evil—may be India is wading through sin and corruption towards peace and progress. But as far as the eye of prudence, prophecy or foresightedness can behold, all is darkness...

As I read the letter in 2013, I cannot help wondering whether the same thought could be expressed today, albeit under a different set of circumstances!

Around 1920, Subhas quit the ICS and joined the national movement. This is when Subhas metamorphosed into Netaji. He seemed focused and single-minded about what he wanted to do. In later years, one of his associates remarked that 'Subhas was a one idea man.'

He led a strike in 1921 when the Prince of Wales visited Calcutta. He was deeply troubled by the 1928 episode in Punjab in which Lala Lajpat Rai died after the police beat him brutally. A young Sikh boy, Bhagat Singh, hurled bombs at the English and was hanged in due course.

In 1930, inspired by the freedom struggle and Netaji, three young men threw bombs at the Writer's Building in Calcutta and shot dead an unpopular and tyrannical Inspector General of Police, Col N.S. Simpson. Benoy Krishna Basu, Badal Gupta and Dinesh Gupta preferred to kill themselves rather than be caught by the English. After India became independent, the famous Dalhousie square was renamed B.B.D. Bagh in their memory.

In 1930, inspired by the Irish uprising of 1916 against the English at Dublin, a group of young people in Chittagong led an uprising at the Chittagong armoury. In due course, the mysterious Masterda, the vivacious Kalpana Dutt and the pensive Pritilata Waddedar were all martyred.

By 1941, Netaji was virtually under house arrest at 38/2 Elgin Road. He summoned his nephew, Sisir Bose, and said to him, '*Aamar ekta kaaj korte parbe?* (Can you do something for me?)' A dramatic plot was hatched for Netaji to escape. One night in 1941, dressed as a Muslim, Netaji was driven by Sisir in their Wanderer 7169 from 38/2 Elgin Road.

After many adventures, including the formation of the Indian National Army at Singapore, Netaji was lost to the nation in an air crash in 1945. The drama continued even after his death when the trial began in Delhi of Sahgal, Dhillon and Shah Nawaz Khan for their activities in the INA.

I used to interact with Balai Dutt of the advertising agency Lintas after I joined the marketing department of Hindustan Lever. He was a seaman in the Royal Indian Navy during the war years. The seamen in the Royal Indian Navy in Bombay and Karachi had revolted in protest against the treatment of Netaji's associates in the Delhi trial. Balai Dutt narrated a first-hand account of the whole story and took me to the memorial set up for the martyrs near the Cooperage in Bombay.

Elgin Road holds a lot of memories for me.

The second story that gripped my young mind was the unbelievable and amazing incident of the Bhowal Sanyasi. The case itself began around 1910 and ended by 1945 before I was born. However, my father, a newcomer to Calcutta in the 1930s, lapped up the stories and reports in the *Amrita Bazaar Patrika* and *The Statesman*. My young mind was fascinated, not only by the story, but also the way in which father narrated it.

There was a zamindari estate in East Bengal called the Bhowal Estate. The patriarch had three sons. This story concerns the second son, Ramendra Kumar Roy, also called the Mejo Kumar, which in Bengali means the middle prince.

Ramendra was brought up lavishly. He would spend the mornings building his body, eat sumptuously, sleep and, in general, indulge in frivolous activities. When he was sixteen, he was taken to a courtesan who did a fine job of inducting Mejo Kumar to the world of eroticism and love. Soon, his life of depravity was common news in the area. To wean him off this path, his mother arranged his marriage with Bibhabati. The ruse was not successful—the marriage never really took off.

Around 1910, Mejo Kumar, Bibhabati and her brother, Satyendra Banerjee visited the hill resort of Darjeeling. Within a few days, the twenty-four-year old Mejo Kumar took violently ill, collapsed and died. There were rumours of food poisoning and of intrigue by the sister-brother duo. However, the facts were never established or proven.

The drama began after that. Some pall bearers were asked to arrange the cremation. They set out with the body and after some time it started raining heavily. The pall bearers returned and reported that their task had been accomplished. The documents of death were prepared by the local authorities in due course and Bibhabati went into the customary mourning. In a few months, Bibhabati moved to Calcutta to live with her brother at 19, Lansdowne Road. This house was a stone's throw from our house at 9, Elgin Road.

A sadhu was spotted around 1920 in Dacca. He resembled the late Mejo Kumar. He did not speak the native Bengali, but Hindi laced with mysticism. Soon, the late Mejo's mother, sister-in-law and many of the locals familiar with Mejo Kumar were convinced that this was indeed the real Mejo Kumar. Apart from physically resembling Mejo Kumar, the sadhu recognized so many places and events that he seemed authentic. After some time, the sadhu declared himself to be the dead person. The late Mejo Kumar's mother accepted him as her son. However, Bibhabati never accepted the sadhu as being the real Mejo Kumar, her husband.

The estate of Bhowal had been in the charge of the government authorities for several years since the three Kumars had all died without heirs. Now the sadhu made a claim on his share of the Bhowal estate. Since Bibhabati never accepted him as Mejo Kumar, a dispute arose. In 1930, a case was filed in the Dacca court by one Kumar Ramendra Narayan Roy.

The case went through the usual legal pyrotechnics. Finally, Justice Pannalal Basu declared that the person claiming to be the second Kumar of Bhowal was really so. There was an appeal in the High Court in 1940. By a majority of two to one, the three-man bench held that the trial court had investigated the subject with a rare thoroughness, and that they found no reason to interfere with its findings. This, though, was not the end of the story.

An appeal was preferred to the Privy Council in London. In 1946, the Privy Council delivered its view that it found no reason to interfere with the earlier decision. The premier Bengali newspaper, *Ananda Bazaar Patrika*, reported a banner headline, 'Council decision in favour of Ramendra Narayan Roy'.

Four days after the Privy Council news, Ramendra Narayan Roy died at the age of 63. The mystery of Mejo Kumar of Bhowal has hung over like a mist since then.

This case resembled the Martin Guerre case, which I read about many years later. Guerre was a sixteenth-century peasant in France. Several years after he had left his wife and child, a man called Martin Guerre appeared in the village. The villagers were convinced that he was the original Martin Guerre. He lived with Madam Guerre and family for three years. Finally, the false Martin Guerre was found out when the real Martin Guerre returned. The false one was tried and executed.

The last narrative that caught my childhood fancy was the Haridas Mundhra scandal. Haridas Mundhra's son was my classmate at St. Xavier's School, and that may have influenced me to follow the case more avidly than any other twelve-year-old would. It was also my first introduction to the unintelligible world of stock markets.

Father had taken us on a tour of the Calcutta Stock Exchange. It housed a number of people called brokers. We did not comprehend a word of what they were shouting to each other, and only ended up arguing whether the language they spoke was Hindi or Bengali! The scam concerned the stock market. I learnt the word 'scam', for the first time and encountered it for years into my adult life!

Haridas Mundhra was a man in a hurry to become rich, an attribute that stood out in the languorous, socialist society of an intellectual, middle-class Calcutta. He lobbied the newly nationalized LIC to buy shares of his companies to prop up their market prices.

It became a scam because this had been done by bypassing the LIC's Investment Committee and the allegation was that there had been a positive signal to do so from Delhi. The person who raised the matter in Parliament was none other than Feroze Gandhi, the son-in-law of Prime Minister Jawaharlal Nehru. Finance Minister T.T. Krishnamachari and Finance Secretary H.V.R. Iyengar were indicted by the Vivian Bose Commission and both resigned.

The film *Sujata* had an evocative song 'Bachpan ke din bhi kya din thay (how wonderful were our childhood days)'. The city that a person grew up in, the school that a person studied in and the stories told by friends and parents are all fond memories for that person alone. However, some memories arise out of a major public event.

I have tried to capture the charm of the times in and around Bengal through the above stories from my childhood. Each of the stories was a personal event for me because of a connection.

Gradually, my brothers, sisters and I moved into adolescence and the family matured—as it happens in all families.

This brief foray into my garden of memories is personal to me. I have indulged myself in the spirit of the Rajesh Khanna song, 'Mere khayalon key aangan mein koi sapnon ka deep jalaye (may someone light up my memories from the garden of my experiences)'.

Maturing into Adulthood

Childhood memories remain etched in a person's mind forever. If the experiences are pleasant, the person must consider his or her situation to be fortunate. These memories are stored in the brain's implicit memory and remembered better than later events as a person advances in age. But then, sure as night must follow day, adolescence must follow the balmiest of childhoods. For me, this happened in the 1960s.

My sister, Jaya, was married in 1954 and by 1961, she was the mother of two boys. We felt great pride in being called *mama* (uncle) as the boys grew up during the 1960s; it made us feel a bit more grown-up than we were.

The next family development was the departure of my elder brother, Raghavan, in 1961. He had graduated in commerce from St Xavier's College and was determined to become a Chartered Accountant like our father, but wished to acquire this qualification in England. I remember my parents discussing how expensive it would be for him to fly out, so they settled for him to go by boat from Bombay. My mother was in a pool of tears after bidding farewell to her son at the quay in Bombay. For several weeks she was inconsolable.

My brother had promised to write a postcard every week as it was too expensive to make an international telephone call, and telegram as a medium of communication was too dramatic and terse. My grandfather, Gopalan, had to content himself with a weekly postcard from his sons in Calcutta. My parents too did likewise, but only that Raghavan's postcard would be an international one. To my brother's credit, he was diligent about writing home as he generally was about all his duties.

My brother had departed with about fifty pounds, as that was the maximum allowed under the prevailing foreign exchange rules. My father had provisionally arranged with a professional firm for Raghavan to do his apprenticeship at five pounds per week. Imagine the shock my parents got when Raghavan wrote a postcard that the firm could not consider him as they had no vacancy, could he try after a year? Raghavan calculated that with his fifty pounds, he could eke out an existence for all of ten weeks. With an obdurate determination that he demonstrated later in life as well, my brother assured my parents that he had no intention of returning. He would stretch every muscle to find an alternative. Was this the Rajam gene at work again?

He succeeded. He trudged to every firm of accountants till he secured his articleship. He qualified as a Chartered

Accountant (England and Wales) and stayed on to gain work experience for almost nine years without ever visiting India. He got married in England to a petite, distant cousin who was also in London. None of us were present at his wedding. Five years later when I got married, my parents decked up the already married couple in wedding clothes and had them photographed for the family records!

Raghavan was, as far as I can recall, the first in our entire extended family to go abroad to study and obtain a professional qualification. His accomplishment became an inspiration to all my cousins and to us. Studying abroad was no more a pipe dream and some of us could aspire for it! Since my parents possessed limited education, that too acquired in small towns, they could not help a frontal display of parental pride on this accomplishment.

Pride is relative to your beginnings. My parents began from a village, so it was understandable.

My sister Saroja was a brilliant student, obtaining a first class and standing first in the university in her BA (Hons) exam! She was the first girl in our entire family from both parents' sides to graduate with a college degree. This was a source of immense pride to my parents. She was a trained Carnatic vocalist as well, but her progress with music was unfortunately cut short by a road accident some years later.

She loved writing, as did my mother. In later years, Saroja became a prolific writer of middles in the *Indian Express*.

The fine arts of writing, speaking and acting were probably the legacy of my maternal grandfather, Karur Soundara Rajan.

Saroja was considered beautiful by a growing band of suitors, some of whom were my contemporaries. This development prompted my mother to go on high drive to find an alliance for her lest she should fall in love with a stranger from a different community! 'Love marriage' was not acceptable to my mother. Such were the times. Saroja got married to Sathyam, a dashing IAS officer, in 1962. Sathyam's family had been as thoroughly checked as his family must have checked out ours.

My father accepted a job in Bombay in 1962. So, by the end of that year, the large family dispersed, as must happen to every family at some stage. My sisters were married, my elder brother was in England and my two younger brothers accompanied my parents to the busy metropolis of Bombay to continue their schooling in the famous Cathedral School.

I stayed back in the St. Xavier's Christian hostel in Calcutta because transferring to Mumbai would have disrupted my academic continuity. I had completed my first year of BSc and would graduate at the age of eighteen in the next two years. Kids all around me, including myself, seemed to be in a hurry to demonstrate precociousness by accelerating studies and becoming earning members of the family.

I was sixteen and all by myself in Calcutta. Since I had to stay back in the college to continue my studies, my father assigned me the concurrent task of settling a court case regarding the house, auctioning the furniture and depositing the sale proceeds in the local bank. This was not what my peers were doing, so I did it a bit reluctantly.

I had to build a relationship with diverse characters like the lawyer, the auctioneer, the court officials; I succeeded in gaining a rudimentary understanding of the issues involved and figuring out the best solution. Telephones between Calcutta and other cities did not work too well in the early sixties, so the frequency of parental consultation was minimal.

But I learnt a lot out of that experience—responsibility, taking charge and understanding complex matters sufficiently enough to act. Such opportunities are commonplace in everybody's life and there is much to be learnt by handling them diligently rather than dealing with them casually or as a burden to be discharged at the earliest possible date.

I studied in a Jesuit school, St. Xavier's, run by Belgian priests and, of course, staffed with many Indian teachers. The school was founded by Belgian Jesuits in 1860 in a discarded theatre on Park Street where it still flourishes. I recall that the school boasted alumni like H.S. Suhrawardy, Siddhartha Shankar Ray and Jyoti Basu, all of whom became Chief Ministers of Bengal in due course. Another luminary who studied at this school was Rabindranath Tagore, India's first Nobel Prize winner. I have many abiding memories about my school teachers, but two bear special mention.

The first was my Sanskrit teacher, Father Antoine. He was a Sanskrit scholar of no mean accomplishment. He taught me for three years. The discipline of Sanskrit grammar, the technique of expressing new ideas by conjoining simple words and the converse of disassembling the *sandhi* (conjoint) by parsing its constituents were all fascinating. I still remember some of the basics, which occasionally help me to understand our old scriptural writings partially.

Father Antoine also taught us about a unique Indian inheritance called *swikriti*. This means the ability to accept an alternate point of view without necessarily agreeing with it or judging it. As I later read in Professor Amartya Sen's writings, *swikriti* represents the equity of tolerance—a very elegant expression. *Swikriti,* according to Father Antoine, was a unique inheritance of Indians, coming down the centuries. 'It would be what will hold India together,' he would say.

The true nuance of Father Antoine's statement came back to me several decades later. India is a rare example in the world of multiculturalism. Every new culture or religion was welcomed and, more importantly, was free to maintain a separate identity. Assimilation did not mean homogenization. Thus, Jews, Christians, Muslims and Zoroastrians coexisted without losing their sense of identity.

At the beginning of the twentieth century, Europe was cosmopolitan. Ideas and nationalities intermingled in a hotbed of creativity, and there were large communities of what were called *passeurs* between multiple European cultures. *Passeurs* was the European equivalent of *swikriti*. However, there was an underlying attempt to homogenize. When Giuseppe Garibaldi united Italy, only two per cent of the population spoke the same language or dialect. He unified Italy by creating the 'new Italian'. Something similar happened in Bismarck's Prussian Germany too.

At the beginning of the twenty-first century, it appears to me that each European nation has become more protective and inward-looking with regard to immigrants, language, culture and trade. Heads of government like David Cameron, Angela Merkel and Nicolas Sarkozy all warn that the trend of encouraging diverse cultures to live side by side has damaged national identity and helped to radicalize immigrant youth. Even the Council of Europe has backed this stand on multiculturalism as a failure, warning that it poses a threat to security. European *swikriti* may well be on the wane.

The second lesson I learnt at school was with respect to learning languages. For some strange reason, I studied as many as four languages—English, Sanskrit, Bengali and Hindi. In addition, my mother coached us in our native Tamil at home. That was quite a load of languages. The outcome was that I could speak several languages quite well when I was young. I even took two years of optional German, studying *Deutsche Sprachlere für Ausländer,* both *Grundstufe* as well as *Mittelstufe,* at the Calcutta Max Mueller Bhavan!

But the struggle was with Hindi. It emerged as my first language for the Higher Secondary school leaving exam. I had to study high-level Hindi literature by well-known essayists like Hazari Prasad Dwivedi and poets like Jaishankar Prasad and Harivansh Rai Bachchan. My overall academic score was always lowered by my lousy performance in Hindi.

One day, my Hindi teacher, Ram Sewak Pande, admonished me. He made the ludicrous suggestion that I converse at home in Hindi. My father, whose Hindi was highly suspect, completely disagreed. He mirthfully remarked that whatever little Hindi I had learnt would also be forgotten if the conversationalist was to be my father!

But as a quid pro quo, he allowed me to see several Hindi films like *Insaaniyat, Sujata, Mughal-e-Azam* and *Madhumati*. The 1950s and 1960s were the decades when Hindi film music followed the traditions of classical music. Great songs like 'Pyaar kiya to darna kya', 'Dil tadap tadap ke keh raha hai' and 'Saranga teri yaad mein' brought cheer to us. Surprisingly, these songs are favourites even with my children's generation. From the 1970s, pop music influence on film music became evident.

The incident remains in my memory because I learnt Hindi by rote, aided by copying things repeatedly. I thought that this might help me to score high. It worked. I think I stood second in Hindi in the school leaving exams. To this day, I can speak chaste Hindi of a much higher quality than many other urban contemporaries. I consider this to be one of my early accomplishments in overcoming obstacles and coming out a winner.

After my graduation, I obtained admission to what was then (and probably still is) India's premier IIT, Indian Institute of Technology, Kharagpur. Like everything else in Bengal, this institute too had a revolutionary history.

It was built around an old jail at Hijli. The jail compound was about a hundred and fifty yards long and about fifty yards wide. Adjacent to it was a hospital. In 1931 there was some commotion in the jail accompanied by firing of bullets. Two innocent spectators from the hospital, Tarakeshwar Sengupta and Santosh Mitra, were killed. Their martyrdom is evocatively memorialized through a walk-around museum. IIT Kharagpur, started in 1951, was also India's first IIT.

During my college graduation, Father de Bonhome taught us physics. He was so good that I took physics as my honours subject. I was fascinated by electromagnetic waves and the very nascent solid state physics. Hence, I opted to study my engineering degree in a relatively infant and obscure branch, at that time called ECE (Electronics and Communication Engineering). I never imagined that several decades later, it would emerge as the most sought-after branch of technology studies.

I should not fail to mention the first winds of international influence that wafted towards me in the prevailing, inward-looking socialist era. I managed access to *Time* magazine at IIT albeit with some difficulty. It opened up a new world of democracy, capitalism, big business, economic progress and student activism to my innocent mind.

By the mid-1960s, the comfortable lifestyle of the baby boomer generation in the West and the Vietnam War gave adequate reason for students all over the world to agitate against the drift in society. London School of Economics and Oxford University held debates on alternate means of non-violence and protests for change. Daniel Cohn-Bendit was a student activist in France and Germany. At Berkeley, students staged a protest against the authorities' restrictions on political activism on the campus, a movement which came to be known later as the Free Speech Movement. India followed with the Naxal movement under the leadership of Kanu Sanyal. The 1960s was an era of turmoil and upheaval everywhere.

1966 was also a seminal year marking the long standing soft influence of Indian art and culture on the West—Professor Joseph Nye termed this as soft power. Sitar maestro, Pandit Ravi Shankar, shot to global acclaim when he taught the Beatniks how to play the sitar. Yoga expert and exponent, B.K.S. Iyengar, arrived in Los Angeles to tutor Hollywood film stars. The Carnatic music nightingale, M.S. Subbulakshmi, was invited by U.N. Secretary General, U Thant, to sing in the United Nations at New York. She enthralled the world with her rendering of 'Saroja Dala Netri' in the Kamboji ragam. All of my siblings matured into adulthood during the tumultuous 1960s.

Joining Hindustan Lever

As I embarked on my final year at IIT, the fact that graduation day was not far away loomed large in my mind. What should one do after graduation? Go abroad, as many classmates were planning, or stay on in India? Study more or work?

I was actually quite fond of my subject of study. Despite several extracurricular activities, I did have an academic bias in contemplating the future. However, due to my preoccupation with the student's gymkhana elections, I had not applied to the US universities in good time. One day, Professor G.S. Sanyal, Head of the Electronics Department, asked me whether I wanted to be recommended for an 'additional scholarship' by the local Rotary Club. On enquiry, I was told that the additional scholarship was offered to the eastern region of the country only once in five or six years. Apart from the usual roster of high accomplishments that one needed, a unique feature of the additional scholarship was that the student would have to study at a college where no Rotary Scholar had ever studied before. This unusual condition put a new light on the opportunity.

I delved deep into the exercise of isolating US colleges where no Rotary Scholar had ever studied. My ambitions of studying at Princeton, Stanford, Purdue and other Meccas of the newly emerging science of electronics were dashed early in the exercise. I ploughed through various directories before arriving at a list of US colleges where no Indian had been before. The most suitable among them, based on personal benchmarks, turned out to be a college in Oklahoma State with the unseemly name, Slippery Rock. If Slippery Rock College was the best I could get to with an 'additional scholarship', I was in deep trouble! I quickly concluded my search and decided that I would not pursue further studies in the US—at least not in the immediate future.

Within the electronics industry, the situation ahead was distinctly worrying. There were government institutions like the Atomic Energy Establishment, Bhabha Atomic Research Centre, Bharat Electronics, etcetera. Somehow, I did not feel motivated to join government departments or companies. It is possible that since my father himself was a professional manager in the private sector, I could have developed a predilection for the same.

Within the private sector, there were basically two companies of repute: Philips India and IBM. I had friends in Philips through whom I gathered that Philips paid very poorly. So that left IBM, where several Kharagpur graduates had joined earlier; and then there were a host of smaller, lesser known electronics companies. It was becoming clear to me that while

I had found my academic curriculum interesting because of the sheer novelty of the subject of electronics (transistors were invented by Shockley just fifteen years earlier!), the development of the industry in India was comparatively slow.

8 January 1967 was a languorous Sunday in the Vidyasagar Hostel. I was reading *The Statesman* in the students' common room when my eye chanced upon an advertisement of Hindustan Lever Limited, asking for management trainees for their Systems department. Their preference was for engineering graduates. The department was new; it would have something to do with making the company more efficient and the prospects were described as 'bright'. The only typewriter I could access was in the technology students' gymkhana. I spent an hour preparing and posting the application, and then forgot all about it.

Things moved rapidly thereafter. By early March, I received an inland letter from one N.L. Mirchandani, with a request to appear for an interview at their Calcutta office. The office was in Ilaco House, a very prestigious building on Brabourne Road. I had once visited an office in that area and returned with the youthful desire to work in one of those buildings.

I was in for a rude shock when I entered Ilaco House. There were posters, graffiti and every possible disfiguring mark colouring the walls. Obviously, HLL was having some problems with the staff union, as there was slogan shouting and wearing of black badges. What sort of a company had I applied to, I wondered.

The interview, a preliminary one as they explained to me, was conducted by a handsome man, G.M. Row, and N.L. Mirchandani from Personnel. It lasted about half an hour. The highlight of the interview, as far as I can recall, was my candid response to a question, 'Do you know what is Organization and Methods, O&M for short?' I said I had definitely heard about the term from some management magazine that my father would bring home periodically, but for the life of me, I could not recall what O&M was all about. I took the train back to Kharagpur, quite certain that I had muffed the interview.

Late in February, the whole campus was abuzz with preparations for the annual spring festival. This was IIT Kharagpur's big socio-cultural event each year. Students from REC Durgapur, Loreto Calcutta, Loreto Lucknow, and so on would spend a week participating in inter-collegiate events such as drama, debating, music, etcetera. It was also the season when many cross-college romances would begin under the benign gaze of the old Hijli jail. As vice president of the gymkhana, I was a busy man.

A telegram from Bombay was delivered to me. Could I please appear for a final interview at Hindustan Lever House in Bombay? I would be paid first class rail fare both ways, but there were just three days in which I had to leave. Wow, first class!

Naturally, I was greatly excited. Here was a company I had applied to quite casually, I had supposedly muffed the first interview, and they were inviting me to Bombay! I had to find a way to extricate myself from the Spring Festival preparations and make the trip to Bombay.

HLL House in Bombay was very, very impressive. I borrowed a suit from my classmate, P. Viswanathan, and took a taxi from Warden Road. This was the best sartorial turnout I had ever undertaken up until then.

HLL House was clad in sheer marble, with huge murals on both sides of the entrance to the building. As I was to learn later, the building was occupied only in 1966, and was built on the spanking new Backbay Reclamation land. We were taken to the board room on the fifth floor, a huge expanse of underutilized office space, and were informed that the Chairman, Mr Prakash Tandon, was seated on one side while the Vice Chairman, Mr R. Ramaswami sat on the other. Next to them sat five other Directors: Scott Birnie, the Managing Director, the Commercial Director Ronnie Archer, Vasant Rajadhyaksha, the Technical Director and the Research Director, Dr S. Varadarajan. Aspie Moddie, the Resident Director, also had an office, though his base was Delhi.

The place was spooky. Nobody seemed to make any noise; those who spoke to us used hushed tones lest it disturbed the gods at work on the floor. There were nine of us. The routine for the whole day was explained and—believe it or not—the outcome was to be announced at the end of the same day. Coming from a college in back-of-beyond Kharagpur, I was struck by the clinical cleanliness of the building and the apparent sense of discipline and reverence of time.

We were interviewed (and watched), by Scott Birnie; Ranjan Banerjee, the Head of Personnel; Vasant Patankar, the Head of Management Services; and Chanderpal Mahimker, the Joint Personnel Manager. As though this 'army' was not enough, a fifth person wearing dark glasses was also introduced as part of the panel. He was, they said, a psychologist named Dr Patel—a consultant with the company.

There were two group discussions, during which time, the five panel members moved about, presumably to get a better view of the participants' visages. Many years later, when I would sit on final selection boards, the logic and value of such a methodology became clear to me. But at that time, it did look like a circus without an agreed ringmaster!

During the sumptuous lunch with the interview panel, I was careful not to spill food on my borrowed suit, or lob the cucumber pieces onto my conversation partner while poking at them with my fork. How I longed to eat comfortably with my fingers like I did at IIT! The private dining room looked far too elegant for me to even entertain such a thought, let alone actually do so!

During the interview, Scott Birnie asked me whether I would consider joining as a Marketing Trainee instead of a Systems Trainee. 'What would that mean?' I enquired with the natural innocence of a caveman who had not been to an institute of management. Once the tasks were clarified, I replied emphatically in the negative. After studying physics and electronics, there was no way I would be seen visiting shopkeepers to sell Dalda or Lux.

'But can you sell at all?' Scott Birnie persisted. I tried to sell him a pencil. Perhaps I did not make a complete fool of myself because he said, 'If you ever change your mind, and wish to come into marketing in the future, do remember to tell somebody.' It was the first inkling I had that maybe, just maybe, they would hire me.

The interview with Dr Patel, the psychologist, was a one-on-one affair. He was blind, I learnt. His questions were most unusual. 'Do you have a girlfriend? Have you kissed her? Draw a tree for me.' Who was this guy, a voyeur or something? I could not assess what he was getting at, but felt reasonably sure that he would declare me to be a hypochondriac, or a schizophrenic or some such head-shrinker's condemnation.

It was 5 p.m. and I was to leave from the Victoria Terminus railway station by the Calcutta Mail at 7.30 p.m. We were informed that three of us had been selected—a direct recruit called Anil Ranadive and two trainees, Dilip Katdare and myself. The undoubtedly dejected candidates were dispatched after a pep talk while the three of us were asked to accompany a Mr Pavshe to the personnel department on the second floor.

Could we please stay back for the medical test the next day? I replied that I would find it difficult to do so, elated though I was by my success. Spring festival was waiting for me, and it was a two-day train journey to Kharagpur. 'Okay, we will fly you down tomorrow evening after the medical test,' they replied.

Wow! Fly me down! This was almost too good to be true, following as it was on my first class train ride. I agreed without batting an eyelid. A dapper young doctor, Ramnik Parekh, did my medicals and declared me fit, save colour blindness. I didn't know what colour blindness was until then! By 3 p.m., the company had me sitting in a chauffeur-driven Dodge on the highway to Santa Cruz airport.

I often wonder about the poor, nameless labourers who selflessly build roads for others to travel on and to dream of their future with hope in their hearts and ambition in their eyes. For me, it was a fantastic ride on Bombay's western express highway. I savoured every moment of it.

I joined the company and for the next thirty-one years, and thereafter for fifteen years in Tata, I savoured every moment of my career, much like that first ride in a chauffeur-driven Dodge.

Lessons from Experience

Both my professional experiences and the personalities I encountered over forty-five years are still fresh in my memory at the time of writing this book. However, I am hesitant to reflect or write about these in any depth lest this manuscript become autobiographical. I would rather share brief narratives about professional incidents, and the lessons that I learnt from them: the lessons of experience.

You have to manage yourself before trying to manage other people or large enterprises—manage your physical self, your mental self and your happiness. This message is elementary, but the most easily forgotten among corporate executives. I learnt this valuable lesson in many memorable ways.

At age nine, I was among the tennis trainees at former Davis Cup player Dilip Bose's coaching scheme at the South Club, Calcutta. We were eager to hit the ball and start playing. He would make us perform fitness exercises for such an extended period of time that we would feel too tired to play. 'If you have only one car to use all your life, you would take the greatest care of it, wouldn't you? Your body is the only car you will have. Learn to take care of it,' he would repeatedly drill into us.

After seven years of service in Hindustan Lever, I became conscious of office politics, though I had no personal experience of it. A distributor at Pune was reported to have black-marketed the company's product, Dalda, at a time when the product was in short supply. I was deputed to investigate and report. I was advised by some experienced company colleagues that it would be a delicate task as I would have to balance between the National Sales Chief (who was thought to favour the distributor) and the Director (who was perceived to dislike the distributor). As I delved into the subject, I found it to be sufficiently complicated by itself. The thought that I had to align my report to handle the so-called sensitivity between the National Sales Chief and the Director did not make sense to me. My middle-class training told me to ignore the politics, if any, and to do my job. And that is exactly what I did, though not without huge pangs of psychological anxiety. Perhaps I was lucky—it all worked out. In fact, my objective report was applauded and I received recognition soon after that.

After three decades at Hindustan Lever, I was explicitly told that I was one in a two-horse race to become CEO of the company. Of course, I thought my credentials were superior. After several months, the Unilever director in charge told me ever so sensitively that the company had selected the other person. He did so at the beginning of a Unilever conference at the seaside resort of Carthagena, Colombia. I was crushed;

I could not enjoy Colombia. I had never missed a promotion compared to my peers in thirty years. I was disappointed, but not devastated. My happiness got disrupted, but only temporarily.

As my tennis coach had told me, you have not lost till the last point is over. I had learnt early that the key to your happiness must always remain in your hands, and never with anyone but you. In due course, I had four job offers to choose from. I retired early from Hindustan Lever to start on what turned out to be a wonderful second career with Tata with a fabulous set of challenges and a great team of professionals to work with.

Another lesson I learnt was that nobody imparts knowledge of soft subjects like humility, empathy and ambition. If you do not prepare your mind to learn these from commonplace experiences, then you alone will suffer the consequences. I have seen so many senior level managers suffer these.

When senior salesman, R.S. Kelkar, travelled with me in the Nashik territory to train me in market management and sales techniques, he told me that I should learn about human management. One evening he took me to the Rama temple at Nashik. He asked me whether I knew why the entrance at many temples was so low that one had to bend to enter. He went on to explain that the message was a reminder to always *namratha dhar* (be humble).

It is human to be ambitious. But how do you know that your ambition has run ahead of your competence? You are never sure. After five years of corporate service in the IT department, when I wanted to move into marketing, my bosses insisted that I retrain at the grassroots level in sales tasks. I was offended at having to take up this job. My boss advised me to deserve before I desired!

On another occasion I argued with my boss that I should be promoted. He simply said that I would be ready to be promoted when I knew more about the subject I was handling compared to any other person. Was I ready to demonstrate that I was ready? Considerably chastened, I withdrew and awaited my turn.

In later years, I was travelling in Ludhiana with N. Sud, a senior salesman. After a morning session in the markets, I informed him that his work was not good enough. He politely requested me to demonstrate 'better' in the market that afternoon. I was angry and humiliated, but also challenged. Fortunately, the company training had included personally doing market work. I did what I had to but obviously not with the panache of Sud's experience. The incident taught me that no boss can expect work from a subordinate if he/she cannot empathise. The boss must experience the pangs of frustration or ecstasy that the subordinate experiences day in and day out before passing judgment summarily.

It is also good to keep a sense of humour and not take yourself too seriously. I was doing an intensive market check on the effectiveness of the sales story communicated for a high powered detergent called OMO. The intended communication was that even if you tied your clothes in a knot, the detergent was strong enough to penetrate the knot and clean the fabric. Imagine my chagrin when the communication played back to me was that the detergent would be effective only if the consumer first tied the clothes into knots before soaking in the detergent!

Through the years, I have found that many corporate conferences and discussions relate to mentoring by seniors. Huge communication and training effort goes into training seniors to be mentors. Nobody tells the mentee that he or she should want to be mentored. Such mental preparation helps a mentee to learn from the advice which falls all around any person like gentle raindrops.

After my graduation in 1964, when I was just over eighteen, my college recommended me to the then famous Calcutta shipping firm, Mackinnon Mackenzie. I completed three rounds of interviews successfully and felt reasonably sure that they would offer me a prestigious traineeship at the princely salary of 450 rupees per month. The final interview was with the CEO, an avuncular person named Mohi Das. He told me that if my family needed me to work, I could have the job. However, he advised me to study further to prepare myself for a 'different working world compared to the one where I worked'. Mohi Das was a mentor, whether or not he intended it. Many years later, I narrated this story to Mohi Das's daughter whom I met at Coonoor.

Alpha-arguing was a valued skill in HLL. With hindsight, I conclude that I grew in Hindustan Lever partly because I developed into an alpha-arguer. During the 1980s, a London-based Unilever colleague described his unique experience with HLL executives in the following light-hearted but realistic terms:

'One of my first impressions was the intense competitiveness of life in India. From just surviving, to not being too polite in a queue (otherwise you would never get in) to a test match in the then Bombay to observing the energy in a HLL workshop where everyone, all high potential executives, spoke at once and no one listened to anyone. But each person had the talent and self-confidence to summarize his own views at the plenary session as the group's view. None of the colleagues questioned the accuracy of it as a summary of their discussion as they did not really know what the group had decided most of the time. I had never seen that before. The other factor beneath the surface, which I came to recognize as a characteristic of life in India then, was the "just carry on in the face of adversity and ignore the obstacles" attitude. You may recall that we had a power failure during one of my presentations with overhead transparencies. A lad arrived with a lantern and I continued in pitch darkness with someone shining the lamp onto the black board. Every so often, a disembodied hand would appear in the arrow of light to either write or rub out a 'keyword' from my presentation.'

For many years seniors would tell younger people to learn to listen. The company sent us regularly on courses like 'Presentation Skills' or 'How to be more persuasive'. I have never come across a course on how to listen better. Ironically, I found very valuable lessons in a paper authored by a Bruno

Kahne, a consultant who taught hearing-impaired children to listen better!

Many of us take notes as we listen to people so that we can remember things. Some of us are not fully engaged with the speaker. On the other hand, deaf people look at the speaker in the eye and make sure that they are fully present in the interaction. They absorb more and retain more, according to Bruno Kahne.

In many management situations, and certainly in television debates, there are simultaneous and multiple conversations. That will never happen with deaf people. They follow a strict protocol of one person speaking at a time. Consensus and agreement are reached faster than out of a heated and overlapping conversation. 'In the long term, slower is faster,' writes Kahne.

Deaf people are direct and they communicate with their thoughts and feelings. They do not hide behind flowery words. They are economical about the way they communicate. For the same reason, they listen well too.

Ask to repeat if you do not understand. Because sign language is much more evolving than the spoken word and signs used by people from one region may be different from those used by people from another region. Deaf people do not hesitate to ask for clarification if they have not understood something.

Deaf people do not multitask, they concentrate on the interaction on hand. They cut themselves off from distractions.

With the advent of PDAs and BlackBerrys, people with normal hearing abilities do the opposite.

A great lesson I learnt was about the key role of intuition in a leader's decision-making. As the newly appointed head of Unilever Arabia, one of my challenges was to mount a frontal attack on a ninety per cent detergent share of P&G. In Arabia, P&G was huge, you did not mess around with their muscle and strength. Unilever did.

The plan was to launch a concentrated detergent to disrupt the market. All the analytical evidence was in favour of this unusual entry mode. My instinct was exactly the opposite. After great hesitation I arrived in London to persuade two main board members to launch with a normal detergent rather than the concentrate. It was not easy to discuss intuition against the data, but to their credit, they listened and blessed the revised approach.

When the family was in Saudi Arabia, we had an unusual experience. In December 1992, the Babri Masjid incident had happened in India. Consequently, Jeddah was tense. Unknown to me, a delegation of supplicants had petitioned the Royal Court that high-paid Hindus like me (ten corporate leaders were named) should be expelled from the kingdom because 'these people send their earnings to India to help destroy mosques'.

The king wisely asked that we be trailed and watched for any nefarious activities for six months. For the period thereafter I had the uncomfortable experience of being tailed by a security officer in mufti. I learnt how mere appearance or religious denomination can end up treating a person like a suspect or an accused.

I wish to recount my experience of working with Ratan Tata and the Tata group. Before I joined the business, I had learnt that in any extrovert business crowd, one might not even notice Ratan Tata's presence, he is so low profile and self-effacing. That he is. But amazingly, there are some people you notice precisely for this reason. I wish to focus on just one of his many attributes. It is the one that leaps out in any discussion with him, irrespective of whether you agree or disagree with his point of view. He is easily the most out-of-the-box thinking business leader I have worked with during my forty-five-year career. He thinks design and not just analytics. When he views a situation or object, he seems to ask, 'What is this part of?' rather than the more commonly asked question, 'What is inside this?' He views an issue holistically rather than in its parts. He is able to activate the tracks of fibers that run from our brain stem all over the body, simultaneously and with equal felicity.

My first example relates to a business acquisition. There was an intense board meeting at which the CEO was presenting an acquisition opportunity. All the directors were fully engaged and were enquiring about all relevant aspects about the market, the synergy, the pricing and so on. At an advanced stage of the discussion, sensing the passion of the management, Ratan Tata said, 'You folks come through as if this is your dream acquisition and that this target company almost perfectly fits with your strategic plan. If my understanding is right, then get on a plane to New York and do not return till you have done the deal.' And that is what happened.

Here is a second example. Soon after I joined Tata from Unilever in 1998, naturally, I was trying to improve my understanding of the Tata Group. In 1999, the Kargil war broke out. Several companies announced their contributions to the war effort and the newspapers were full of photo-ops to mark such corporate giving. I was concerned that Tata would not be seen as responding. So I spoke to Ratan Tata.

His response was matter-of-fact, but became hugely impactful in course of time. 'We need to think about what to give, but also about how to reach it to those for whom it is meant,' he said. He was, of course, referring to the hard reality that in both philanthropy and duty, it is easier to write a cheque than to institutionalize the emotional commitment that must accompany such giving. Over the next six months, he personally convened meetings of group leadership and I was fortunate to be a participant.

What emerged at the end was extraordinary. The employees, the operating Tata companies and the Tata Trusts together raised a corpus, which I had calculated at that time to be in excess of the contribution of the top twenty-five public companies put together. Most uniquely for those days, a bespoke Defence Tata Welfare Corpus was established to disburse the interest from the corpus to deserving cases. It had three trustees from Tata, and one each from the army, the air force and the navy.

The Trust had seventeen meetings over the next ten years. On the advice of senior defence officers, the Trust was mandated to help not only Kargil victims, but also the victims of the earlier wars of 1965 and 1971. There was no press release, photo-op or information to the outside world.

This way of doing philanthropy seemed to be 'Do what you have to do, and do not worry about the credit.' I did not expect to see it so palpably in the busy world of business.

The third episode occurred in 2001. It was approaching midnight and I was at a dinner party when my cell phone rang. It was from a journalist, who was tipping me off about an anonymous letter doing the press rounds, referring to some wrong-doings in Tata Finance. I called Vice Chairman Noshir Soonawala in spite of the late hour. He had already been woken by another caller. Leaders of the group like Noshir Soonawala and Ishaat Hussain were quickly assembled by Ratan Tata. Their mandate was to study the matter and deal with the issues with total openness. Their team had his active guidance.

In the early days, the nature and extent of the damage were both fuzzy and extremely worrying. During this period, there was a Tata Chemicals Annual General Meeting of shareholders. Although Tata Finance was not an appropriate subject for this meeting, some elderly shareholders wailed with great emotion that they stood to lose their limited savings in Tata Finance.

To my astonishment, Ratan Tata stood up and boldly announced that Tata would stand behind every small investor. Nobody needed to fear losing their valuable and hard-earned savings. I was stunned that a business leader could be so empathetic and make such a public commitment. He instinctively acted on the principle that when there is a crisis, you just have to do what your sense of duty and conscience dictates.

For me that is Ratan Tata: an out-of-the-box thinker, an embodiment of creativity, responsible leadership and humanism in a rare cocktail. I am privileged to have closely worked with this unusual leader.

The narratives and lessons over forty-five years can continue endlessly. However, I must stop lest the book stray into a management book. I included a few episodes only to round off the humour, emotion and memories of a career that I greatly enjoyed.

LPR to LPG in the Twenty-First Century

Exactly half of my professional career was spent in the infamous licence-permit-regulation (LPR) regime, and the second half in the liberalization-privatization-globalization (LPG) regime. During these periods, significant changes occurred in educational, social, and employment opportunities as India entered the twenty-first century. I often reflected on what they would mean for my children's generation.

When I was studying, there was a mad rush for admission into the IITs. Whether one studied in an IIT or not, a very large proportion of the bright students studied engineering. During the 1980s, there was a proliferation of engineering colleges all over the country, especially led by the southern states.

A fair proportion of IIT engineering graduates pursued further studies, mostly in North America. Of those who went abroad, a large proportion of engineers stayed on to pursue a career there. India lost perhaps two-fifths of her brightest IIT engineering graduates to the USA during the last half-century.

At the age of thirty-five, my former classmates in America would be owning a comfortable flat or house, driving an air-conditioned Pontiac or Ford car with savings to boot. I was thirty when I bought my first car, and that too, I must admit needed some help from my father. Riding an air-conditioned car was a luxury that I realized only when I was over forty. Savings began only when I was posted abroad during my career. I was forty-five before I owned any property. Our next generation achieved these milestones much earlier.

Throughout the first half of my LPR career, almost every modestly capable young man would endeavour to somehow escape the gravity of the Indian economy and catapult into foreign air space, whether to North America, Europe or even the Middle East. During the latter half of my LPG career, even those who went to study abroad had returned to seize the greater opportunities emerging in India. Except for a couple of our next generation, every grandchild of Rajam has returned after studying abroad.

Another attractive career option for young people was to study accountancy, mostly in the UK. A generation of accountants stayed to practise and work abroad. I am unable to estimate the numbers India lost; suffice to say it would not be small.

Studies in private sector business started to take shape about the time I completed my academic career. Until the 1960s, children followed their fathers' careers. Army kids joined the army, bureaucrats' children joined the IAS or the IPS, and so also with lawyers and doctors. Thanks to a strongly socialist regime from 1947, the private sector was kept on a leash by an overbearing regime of government planning and controls. Hence, there were very few managers in the private sector and so the question of following your father into management did not arise at all.

Among my contemporaries in Hindustan Lever, I was among a minority who was a second-generation manager.

During the 1960s, two IIMs were established. For the first time, the possibility arose of studying and practising management as a profession. Soon, IIT MBA graduates began to embark on a management or financial services career with little connection to their technical education. Just as the nation lost technical talent to countries abroad, the nation lost engineers to the new-fangled profession of management.

Today there is a proliferation of management colleges all over the country. MBAs from India can boast of being part of the largest output of MBAs in the world, even though their quality may rightly be considered dubious! India churns out about 150,000 so-called management graduates through approximately five thousand management colleges. Indore alone boasts of about forty!

The advent of information technology and private sector service industries (like telephony, financial services and media) emerged as career possibilities. This was undoubtedly aided by the country's entrepreneurial LPG regime compared to the suffocating LPR regime. So from the mentality of my father's generation of somehow getting a job, my generation tried to get a good and secure job. But to the next generation, the job market is diverse, offering multiple opportunities. Staying with one employer for any length of time is almost *passé* nowadays.

I can make a startling point about jobs and careers. The number of organized sector (where industrial dispute laws and labour laws apply) jobs in Indian manufacturing and services has remained static for fifty years at about 6.5 million. This is despite the explosion of economic activity since the LPG regime was ushered in. All the employment growth has occurred in what is termed the informal sector.

Leading the pack are the three million professionals in the IT sector, which is expected to cross organized sector employment by 2017 or so. The key reason for this skewed employment pattern may be attributed to the arcane labour laws in the country.

The next generation of the family does not know much about the LPR regime, having had no experience of it. As a result, they find it difficult to believe my generation when we relate how difficult it was to buy milk or secure a cooking gas connection, let alone buy a two-wheeler or car. Compared to my friends in North America, we lived a very austere life right through the first half of my career.

But all that changed for the better with the advent of the LPG regime from 1991, so much for the tremendous changes in the educational and job opportunities.

Another significant change occurred in aspiration and life expectations. Unlike other colonies like Indonesia (which banned the Dutch language after independence), English quite literally became a goddess in India. It was and continues to be seen as a passport to progress by the common citizen. Even in smaller towns, people prefer to send their children to English-medium, private schools rather than the free government-run, vernacular schools.

In Uttar Pradesh, the dalits constructed a temple where the resident deity is a hypothetical goddess called Goddess English. The dalit view was that the upper castes had traditionally excluded them from development by monopolizing Sanskrit. According to them, the upper castes were now excluding dalits by monopolizing the English language. So the study of English has become a fetish for all—not necessarily the Queen's English, but a sort of Hinglish. Author Gurcharan Das narrates his experience at a wayside restaurant in Uttar Pradesh. The young lad serving him kept responding in English to his questions in Hindi. Upon being asked the reason, the youngster replied that he wanted to learn just four hundred words so that he could pass his TOEFL (Test of English as a Foreign Language) exam required to work in America!

The education of women and the number of women at work has also witnessed a big change. My sister was the first woman graduate in our family. Geeta, my wife, has enjoyed a working career, juggling hard between a job and raising our children. Our daughters and daughters-in-law are highly educated and, exceptions apart, pursue a working career as a natural path without considering the alternative of being full-time housewives.

Even my village, Vilakkudi, has changed, although not as dramatically as elsewhere. Compared to my earlier visits, the population has not changed much—from three thousand to four thousand. But that is because the sons of the village have migrated. Electricity and telephones, including cell phones, have appeared. The social structures have adapted to the new reality. However, the warmth of the village and the so-called 'village mentality' is still visible, as illustrated by an amusing incident.

Our family had visited Vilakkudi in 2007. My old uncle Sampath in the village was the only surviving member of my father's cousins. He had largely lived his life in Vilakkudi. He took me aside and asked in an undertone, 'I understand that you have a big job in Mumbai. Your father would have been proud of you if he was alive. What might your salary be? I understand that it could be as much as thirty thousand rupees per month!'

Village folks are always curious about such matters, but I managed to dodge a direct answer. He then followed up with his next question. 'I understand that Geeta is also working in an office. I wonder what her salary would be. Maybe ten thousand rupees per month?' he asked. Not receiving a denial or a confirmation, he sagely advised, 'You should tell her that she need not work. If she managed your earnings well, she could save ten thousand from your handsome salary.'

I narrate this episode because the situation represents the contradictory reality of India. For every individual or family that has become MUL (modern, urban and liberal), there are others on the escalator of economic and social progress, some racing ahead and some struggling to keep pace. Modernity and backwardness, liberal thinking and archaic attitudes coexist in a bewildering juxtaposition that even Indians find difficult to understand, let alone foreigners.

It may be appropriate to mention our next generation.

My parents had no college degree. All their grandchildren have college degrees, prized ones too, from universities such as London, Melbourne, Stanford, Wharton and Harvard. They are all MUL.

My parents had six children and twelve grandchildren. While my parents' children married within the community, almost everyone from the next generation has chosen his or her life partner. Horoscopes are neither considered relevant nor believed in. Of the twelve in-laws we welcomed into the family, we have four religious denominations and only a few have a Tamil Brahmin spouse. Pure and classical Tamil weddings have been celebrated to maintain tradition, but otherwise, family wedding events were invariably accompanied by multiethnic festivities. All urban Indian weddings have acquired a Punjabi touch anyway, with the introduction of *sangeet* and *mehendi* even in the conservative south. The language of communication is more and more Tinglish and Hinglish: 'father is *thoongifying*' (sleeping) or referring to a wife's sister's husband as 'my co-brother-in-law'.

I had an amusing experience with Hinglish when I interviewed a Hindi-speaking veterinarian for my company's dairy in UP. I asked him to explain in simple English what artificial insemination meant. After some deep thought, he said, 'AI is when a man does it to the cow instead of a bull doing it!'

Is all this good or bad? It depends on how you look at it. On balance, a society or nation progresses by adapting subtly to the changes demanded by the wider world. That is how Ooshi reluctantly conceded to the views of a better informed and much-travelled Gopalan; Gopalan reluctantly permitted all his sons to migrate to the cities though he stayed on in the village. Despite his rural background, Rajam became modern and ensured that all his children were prepared for the times ahead. And I would like to believe that my generation has done the same for the following generation. Viewed this way, everything that has happened is progress.

Progress means holding on to the core values and letting go of the frills, accoutrements and symbolisms. That is the subject I would like to explore in my last chapter.

Looking Ahead

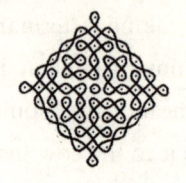

I now approach the end of my narrative covering two hundred years. I sit on the balcony of my Mumbai flat on a humid monsoon evening. I watch the traffic of Cuffe Parade go by, much like Ranganathan on his *thinnai* (porch) watching the goings-on in his *agraharam* in 1850. I am also bothered by the ubiquitous monsoon fly, but I am equipped with a plastic fly swatter and the whirring of a fan instead of an *angavastram* and *vishiri*.

I doze off thinking about the messages from a fascinating book by historian David Priestland entitled *Merchant, Soldier, Sage: A New History of Power*. The author argues that in viewing history, one must distinguish between economic interests (a Marxian motive, power, which is driven by individual and personal gain) and ideological interests (a Fukuyama concept dealing with the values and ideas of groups of people).

I resonate with the values and ideas approach of Francis Fukuyama. That is precisely why I wrote this book. It is all about what *sanskar* (inheritance of values) a person derives from his or her ancestors.

A wiry and athletic group of youngsters jog past noisily, and their laughter breaks my catnap. They are evidence that what Indian society has experienced during the short liberalization-privatization-globalization era since 1991 is one of history's most inspiring and uplifting transformations. The outcome so far is not a picture of perfection. That it has been dramatic cannot be denied. My father was taller than his father. My brothers and I were taller than our father. My son stands a good few inches above me. Britain took one hundred and fifty years to double its per capita income. America took thirty years. India is doubling every eight years.

Caste is a term that the young MUL Indian despises. Society is not the mere sum of the economic interests of atomized individuals. Priestland postulates that society comprises work occupations and occupational groups, each characterized by its own ethos.

The occupation of people is central to the manner in which social groups coalesce and regroup. For example, in the India of the twenty-first century, one can see a new caste emerging. It is not based on the classical model, but on occupation. The new *varna* bears a resemblance to an old system.

New Brahmin sages have emerged: the academics, economic planners, bureaucrats, judges, journalists and professional managers. Their intellect is valued by society. They provide sage advice to the rulers, provide checks and balances to those in power and provide order in a developing and chaotic society.

Then there are the new Kshatriya rulers who command power, sometimes brutally. They offer protection to their loyalists and followers: politicians, land mafias, extortionists and black money operators. Their ruthless tactics to capture and retain power are experienced on a daily basis. They pretend to rule benevolently, but do so only to further their own selfish interests just like the zamindars (landowners) of yesteryear.

The new Vaishya merchant is the restless entrepreneur whose energy and animal spirit are major economic drivers of the country's growth: small-scale industries, rags-to-riches industrialists, commodity and stock market operators and traditional traders. The methods they use to advance their economic interests may sometimes appear suspect, but they are definitely the engines of economic growth. This class allows the politicians to think that they rule, but in reality, they set their own rules which they incentivise the politician to accept.

The new artisanal worker is the factory hand, the government clerk, the farm hand and the employee in the burgeoning service industry.

Finally, there are the new untouchables who yearn for society's attention and sensitivity: the jobless, the landless, the urban migrant worker and the uneducated millions for whom emancipation has been, and looks set to remain, a pipe dream.

The traditional Indian caste system used to be immutable, but not this new caste system. Nowadays, a traditional Brahmin may be a maker or marketer of leather footwear or meat products. A traditional peon or clerk becomes a sage or a doctor. The traditional dalit may be a flourishing, capitalist businessman.

Romans called their caste system *ordine,* medieval Europe called theirs *order,* Bishop Gerard said in 1024 CE, 'From the beginning mankind has been divided into three parts...men of prayer, farmers and men of war.' The Hindus called it *varna.*

Each generation experienced a very busy life, though when looked at with hindsight, it appeared a slow and languorous life. Gopalan experienced the connected world through the train and postcard. Rajam experienced the connected world through radio and television. My generation experienced the connected world of the Internet. There is little doubt that the next generation will experience a hyper-connected world. In the future world, people can start things, learn intensely by themselves and collaborate furiously with an almost unlimited number of people.

Although some people hold the view that values are *passé* or old-fashioned, the lessons I draw from writing the book are exactly the opposite. Some are generic values and some are family-specific values.

When times are turbulent and unpredictable, keeping sight of the shore becomes all the more important. That comforting shore is the continued adherence to values.

The first value exemplified is the art of family conversation. I reflect on how patiently Ranga explained things to an inquisitive Ooshi and how intimate the conversation was between Rajam and his children. Deep conversations are at the heart of family bonding and family bonding is at the heart of social progress. Will the hyper-connected world diminish the art of family conversation?

I worry, much as Ranga worried about Ooshi, Ooshi worried about Gopalan, Gopalan worried about Rajam and Rajam worried about us. It seems unavoidable that each generation should worry about the next! But the next generation does figure out new ways of surviving and prospering.

The second value that comes through is constant and gentle adaptation from a monoculture to a multicultural capability. The twenty-first century social environment also has an *agraharam*, but not one where Brahmins live together. The *agraharams* are of steel men, railwaymen, film stars, equity analysts, merchant bankers, administrators and professional managers.

A new generation of cosmopolitan youngsters is growing up. They think in English, they speak English as a main language, and are often uncomfortable with their native tongue.

Is this good or bad? It does not matter because it is real. The new *agraharams* of such groupings are already visible in the residential apartments of the upscale areas of Cuffe Parade, Malabar Hill and Bandra; in the suburbs of Lokhandwala, Juhu and Versova and in the gymkhanas and clubs of our cities.

The third value that I can identify is the attitude towards education. In my family the hunger for education, especially among women, was a driver of huge change. After all, for centuries, Indians have worshipped Saraswati as the goddess of learning. Middle-class societies all over the world value education as a means to economic and social progress. Our society has a burgeoning middle class. This is fuelling an unprecedented growth in education. The Indian education market has been estimated as being bigger than steel and automobiles put together!

The next generation has a novel response to religion. For the ancestors in Vilakkudi, it was the idol at the Sri Kasturi Ranga temple and the temples of Tanjore. Their prayers would be long and vedic. Now the gods reside in young people's hearts, in small puja corners within a flat, or in the city's public temples. There are short bursts of interaction with their God. My children are least interested in the ritual, but they are eager to preserve the spirit.

My daughters carry a mini Ganesha wherever they travel. My son meditates alone for five brief minutes before he departs for his office everyday. Further, their prayers are multi-denominational in deference to a Christian or Sikh in-law in the family. The next generation is not hung up about visible religious rituals, though most of them are respectful of them.

Some of my nephews and nieces acknowledge a novel form of God called Luck. They actually pray for Luck to guide and help them. It is an implicit acceptance that there is an unknown and mysterious force that matters. Their mantra seems to be what the bard wrote in *Hamlet*: There is a divinity that shapes our ends, rough-hew them how we will.

The fourth value is about leading and leadership. The next generation is certainly inspired by the leadership stories of Gandhi, Nehru and Lincoln. But they are far more influenced by the leadership qualities of their parents, uncles, bosses and contemporary business icons. To them these are real people whose strengths and foibles they have experienced or witnessed. They can learn from the strengths and leave the foibles aside in imbibing what kind of life they would like to lead.

As they watch the news, they recognize what a weak leader looks like. Bahadur Shah Zafar, who was chosen because he was the least unacceptable leader, comes alive. To the next generation, history gets reinforced.

The fifth value concerns a liberal attitude. The ancient value of *swikriti* (each unto his own way), exemplified by Father Antoine's lesson in my school, appeals to the next generation which is intolerant of communal parochialism, especially visible in our politics. That is why they are far more sensitive about incidents like the Sikh killings of 1984, Babri Masjid incident in 1992 and Godhra, 2002. They are prepared to fight on the streets if needed, and we have experienced the force of youth repeatedly, aided by a vigorous media.

The last value that I will touch upon is with respect to public morality and corruption. Based on a global perspective and their inherited *sanskar*, the next generation has a more distinctive view of morality and corruption. It is true that this is a scourge with politicians all over the world: be it the US, Europe, Japan or the South Asian nations. India is part of a worldwide disease.

On some mornings, India's case looks worse and more chronic than others. Without doubt, it is a disease that deserves to be debated and mitigated with urgency. But the young are impatient about waiting. They derive a wee bit of comfort, though reluctantly, when they learn that the US and UK were no different at their equivalent, adolescent stage of economic and social transformation.

In his book, *Merchant Kings*, author Stephen Bown reminds the reader that 'contrary to the portrayal of European Empires as the creation of kings and nation states, private economic interests did as much as statesmen to colonise the globe.' Kings chartered national trading companies with valuable monopoly rights to do business in far-flung lands, thus releasing the temptation toward direct conquest and the display of animal spirits.

Historians seem to agree that 'corruption was endemic in eighteenth century politics, with the sale of office being a widespread phenomenon throughout Europe.' One political theorist portrayed eighteenth-century England as 'shot through with corruption and venality'. It was as late as March 1888 that a Royal Commission in England recommended 'that it would be well if it were made a criminal offence to offer any member or official of a public body any kind of payment...'

Teddy Roosevelt was pessimistic in the early 1900s about America's future when he observed, 'The dull, purblind folly of the very rich men; their greed and ignorance, and the way in which they have unduly prospered...these facts, and the corruption in business and politics, have tended to produce a very unhealthy condition.'

Attitudes and approaches to corruption create anomalies which are difficult to explain rationally. For example, Switzerland regularly tops transparency and low corruption studies. It is a contradiction that clean Switzerland held secret Nazi money during World War II. Nowadays, it is the not-so-secret repository of the most toxic money from all over the world, including some Indians! The Swiss collect this corrupt money at low interest rates and lend it out to the world at high rates—and are rated to be the cleanest society!

The sun is setting into the Arabian Sea and the shadows on Cuffe Parade are lengthening. As I approach the dusk of my own life, the death of my father Rajam flashes into my consciousness.

One Sunday in 1989, my elder brother Raghavan visited father. Father was resting, relaxed and cheerful, but looking a little tired. He requested Raghavan to pass him some medicine. Before the medicine could be handed over, he was gone. Raghavan was taken aback by the suddenness of the incident and shocked by the actual occurrence of the inevitable.

Father left behind my mother, Rukmini, and eighteen children and grandchildren in total. Every member of the clan managed to arrive in time for the cremation.

He moved on from this world with the fondest of farewells from each person in his large, happy family; he died in a trice without suffering or pain. Friends and relatives observed that he had died a contented man after a unique life.

But what was so unique or special about his life? It was the quotidian story of many common people, the story of a small town boy who made a career in the city. He was not a well-known hotshot who had been decorated by the government or who had streets named after him! Surely those are criteria that should determine whether a life is well-spent!

On the other hand, isn't every life unique and special? Every experience teaches a person distinct lessons. Those lessons stay with him and remain uniquely his.

GDP cannot be the only measure of a society's progress. I recall a J.R.D. Tata quote which said that he would rather see a happy India than an economically powered India. How true!

It all comes down to what makes a person happy. The lessons from my ancestors as taught to us were to lead a life worth living, to learn to work without seeking the rewards and to seek happiness from within rather than from outside. It all sounds simple, but billions are trying to learn about happiness everywhere in the world.

I read about the Grant happiness study which followed the developments in the lives of 268 men in the Harvard class of 1937. For seventy-three years the study tracked all areas of their life—physical, social, emotional and professional. This study is the longest 'quality of life' research project ever conducted, and it has been presided over since the 1960s by psychologist, Dr George Vaillant.

Joshua Shenk wrote an excellent article on the findings of the research study in the *Atlantic* magazine. The study traced the lives of the students which include unbelievable changes. Many students who started off brilliantly fizzled out and developed problems; some who began with problems worked on them and died happy old men.

The study identified six variables which contribute to human happiness:

i. education
ii. stable relationships
iii. not smoking or alcohol abuse
iv. warm cohorts: siblings, school friends and others
v. exercise and healthy weight
vi. healthy adaptation.

I feel inspired that these lessons are very visible in the narrative of my ancestors. So if the next generation can be discriminative enough to retain the essence of ancestral values and yet adapt to the emerging circumstances, then my brothers and sisters need not worry about what would happen to them.

I hear some commotion in the drawing room. Preparations are on for a family function in the evening; my nuclear clan has got together. Geeta is busy entertaining herself with our grandchildren—Yash, Shrey and Tiara. My eldest daughter, Anugraha, is admonishing her son to finish his meal, ably assisted by her British husband, Barny Crocker. Our son, Anirudha, and his Punjabi-Goan wife, Nisha, have their hands full trying to keep their two kids in good cheer. Our youngest daughter, Anila, and her husband, Gunteshwar, load the sound system with the right music.

I wonder what the future holds for them. What will it be like in 2050 or 2100? Will they be happy and united? Will they speak Tamil, Hindi, English or Java? Will they ever know about their ancestors from Vilakkudi? Would one of them be interested in writing the story about the next generations?

My ears are filled with the lilt of the memorable Doris Day song from Alfred Hitchcock's 1956 film, *The Man Who Knew Too Much*.

When I was just a little girl, I asked my mother 'What will I be?'
Will I be pretty? Will I be rich?
Here's what she said to me.
Que sera, sera, whatever will be, will be,
The future's not ours to see, Que sera, sera.

Khalil Gibran's moving poem springs to my mind. How sensitive the poet was when he wrote it!

Your children are not your children,
They are the sons and daughters of Life's longing for itself.
They come through you but not from you,
And though they are with you yet they belong not to you.

The greatest treasure that we can leave for our children is not wealth but *sanskar*. The more of us who can do so, the better society will be.

So I bid you adieu, dear reader. May fortune smile upon you. Treasure the unique gift of *sanskar* inherited from your ancestors. Pass the *sanskar* to your children and to your grandchildren.

May the new *karma* called 'que sera, sera' always inspire you.